DIVERSITY OF VOCATIONS

Catholic Spirituality for Adults

General Editor
Michael Leach

Other Books in the Series
Holiness
Prayer
Reconciliation

DIVERSITY OF VOCATIONS

✳

Marie Dennis

Maryknoll, New York 10545

Founded in 1970, Orbis Books endeavors to publish works that enlighten the mind, nourish the spirit, and challenge the conscience. The publishing arm of the Maryknoll Fathers and Brothers, Orbis seeks to explore the global dimensions of the Christian faith and mission, to invite dialogue with diverse cultures and religious traditions, and to serve the cause of reconciliation and peace. The books published reflect the views of their authors and do not represent the official position of the Maryknoll Society. To learn more about Maryknoll and Orbis Books, please visit our website at www.maryknoll.org.

Library of Congress Cataloging-in-Publication Data
Dennis, Marie.
    Diversity of vocations / Marie Dennis.
        p. cm. – (Catholic spirituality for adults)
    ISBN-13: 978-1-57075-716-7
    1. Church work – Catholic Church. 2. Service (Theology)
3. Vocation – Catholic Church. I. Title.
BX2347.D46 2008
248.8'9432 – dc22
                                                    2007042350

Contents

Introduction to
Catholic Spirituality for Adults

C ATHOLIC SPIRITUALITY FOR ADULTS explores the deepest dimension of spirituality, that place in the soul where faith meets understanding. When we reach that place we begin to see as if for the first time. We are like the blind man in the Gospel who could not believe his eyes: "And now I see!"

Catholicism is about seeing the good of God that is in front of our eyes, within us, and all around us. It is about learning to see Christ Jesus with the eyes of Christ Jesus, the Way, the Truth, and the Life.

Only when we *see* who we are as brothers and sisters of Christ and children of God can we begin to *be* like Jesus and walk in his Way. "As you think in your heart, so you are" (Prov. 23:7).

Catholic Spirituality for Adults is for those of us who want to make real, here and now, the words we once learned in school. It is designed to help us go beyond information to transformation. "When I was a child; I spoke as a child, I understood as a child, I thought as a child; but when I became an adult, I put away childish things" (1 Cor. 13:11).

The contributors to the series are the best Catholic authors writing today. We have asked them to explore the deepest dimension of their own faith and to share with us what they are learning to see. Topics covered range from prayer — "Be still and know that I am God" (Ps. 46:10) — to our purpose in life — coming to know "that God has given us eternal life, and that this life is in his Son" (1 John 5:11) — to simply getting through the day — "Put on compassion, kindness, humility, and love" (Col. 3:12).

Each book in this series reflects Christ's active and loving presence in the world. The authors celebrate our membership in the mystical body of Christ, help us to understand our spiritual unity with the entire family of God, and encourage us to express Christ's mission of love, peace, and reconciliation in our daily lives.

Catholic Spirituality for Adults is the fruit of a publishing partnership between Orbis Books, the publishing arm of the Catholic Foreign Mission Society of America (Maryknoll), and RCL Benziger, a leading provider of religious and family life education for all ages. This series is rooted in vital Catholic traditions and committed to a continuing standard of excellence.

Michael Leach
General Editor

Author's Introduction:
A Diversity of Faithful Pathways

WHAT DOES IT MEAN to have a vocation? Is a vocation a job, a career, a way of life? What does money have to do with it? Have you often asked yourself — at twenty, thirty, forty, or sixty — what am I going to do with the rest of my life? You're not alone. Understanding vocation is the key to living life, not in the future but here and now. Understanding vocation is the key to living a meaningful life, the key to fulfillment on life's journey.

John Neafsey, a clinical psychologist and lecturer in the theology department at Loyola University in Chicago, clarifies the issue for us in his book *A Sacred Voice Is Calling*. He says vocation has to do with the "kind of person we are called to be, the quality of our personhood, the values and attitudes we embody, the integrity and authenticity of our lives."[1] Neafsey writes about vocation in a broad, interdisciplinary, and ecumenical sense.

Looking at vocation from another perspective, the *Catechism of the Catholic Church* turns to the Beatitudes, which "express the vocation of the faithful associated with the glory of [Jesus'] Passion and Resurrection; they shed light on the actions and attitudes characteristic of the Christian life."[2]

For Christians, vocation is the invitation to follow Jesus. "Come after me," he said, in the beginning of the Gospel of Mark (1:17), an invitation to discipleship that, "more than an assent of the heart," demands "an uncompromising break with 'business as usual.' "[3]

To write a book about vocations for adults implies, rightly, that discerning one's vocation is a life-long process, requiring a heart finely tuned to the voice of God. It suggests the long-term task of matching the cadence of one's being to the rhythm of God's language.

This little book will explore a few dimensions of vocation. Hopefully, it will spark your own reflections on the topic and open for you a greater depth of meaning in your own life or paint some new challenges and dreams on your horizon.

DIVERSE VOCATIONS

As a high school senior in 1960 I, like many other young women of that day, was convinced that my future was in the convent, but I decided to postpone any commitment to religious life until after college. Four years later, as I graduated from college, I was convinced that marriage was my vocation and that I would give my life to parenting a large and happy family. Ten years later, with five young children (and another yet to come), I was convinced that my calling was also to work for social justice and to participate in the transformation of the world.

When I look back now at the diversity of vocations to which I have been called in the decades that have passed since I finished high school, I am filled with wonder at the love of a gracious God. My vocational pathway never deviated very far from the sisters whose lives inspired me as a young woman. I have witnessed, walked with, been deeply challenged by, lived with women religious in these years. I have a much, much deeper appreciation of their gift to our broken world than I did in school. At the same time, the vocation closest to my heart, the one that shapes my self-understanding and gives deep meaning to my life, is that of mother. Yet woven into the fabric of how I am as a woman of faith and of how I have parented, or tried to parent, my children is the call to be co-creator of a better world.

I have come to understand "vocation" as much more than "state in life": single, married, vowed religious, ordained. My own experience of "vocation" has simply not been that neat, or that linear. One can change vocations, can embody more than one vocation at a time, can discover a new vocation at any time in life. Sometimes, later in life, it's discovering the newness of a vocation we've had for decades but never saw with open eyes.

A few more words about my own journey might help the reader understand the lens through which I am looking at this topic nearly half a century after my decision to grow into my "vocation" by waiting until after college to enter the convent.

Like so many of my peers in the mid-1960s I was married immediately after graduating from college, where I had majored in physics. I worked as a physicist for the U.S. Navy and then spent two years on Guam while my husband served his required time in the Air Force. We were settling in for the long haul with a growing family. My vocation was clear. It never occurred to me then that my life might move in unexpected directions, that in the years to come I would travel to Cambodia and Zimbabwe, El Salvador and Afghanistan, Colombia and Palestine, and perhaps thirty other countries; that I would have breakfast with the president of the United States; milk a cow and make hay; accompany the president of Haiti on his return from exile; sit in vigil outside the White House through long nights on end with Sister Dianna Ortiz, a courageous survivor of torture in Guatemala; watch de-mining teams inch their way through minefields in Afghanistan; sit in meetings with the president of the World Bank and the managing director of the International Monetary Fund; get deported from El Salvador for accompanying refugees back to their land; fast for forty-two days; work on a project with the archbishop of Canterbury; write books; spend time in jail for civil disobedience. I had no idea as I launched into life that taking "the next right step," just saying yes to a still, small voice, would take my life in so many unusual but wonderful directions.

ORDINARY BEGINNINGS

We had settled quickly into raising a family. Three daughters and three sons kept me happy, fulfilled, and very busy as we tried to give them the tools to live loving and faithful lives in a world we began to see as tragically broken by poverty and violence. When the children were all very young we began to feel increasingly uncomfortable with the homogeneity of our upper-middle-class neighborhood and the gap that existed between our family, and the poor of the world. We began to adjust our lifestyle bit by bit to respond to a new "vocation."

We began to replace our grass with vegetable gardens; we turned off the air conditioner, disconnected the dryer, and tried to use other appliances less often. We opened our home and family to foster children and found ourselves ill-equipped to meet the needs of the young teenaged boys who came to stay. Only one was with us for any length of time, and that turned out to be enormously challenging.

Ultimately, we moved, lock, stock, and barrel, to a sixty-five-acre farm much in need of repair and tender loving care. We started from scratch to acquire the skills necessary to grow and preserve food organically, milk a cow, churn butter, care for a wide variety of animals, mend fences, spin and weave, make hay, and run pretty dilapidated farm machinery, learning everything from scratch, appreciating enormously the dignity and wisdom of our neighbors, almost all of whom were dirt poor, literally. Many of the skills I learned in those years tied me to women of all time who had done those same chores, and especially to impoverished women around the world who do or who yearn to do so now.

The children jumped into farming with enthusiasm, learning valuable lessons about nurturing life, accepting responsibility, facing death, and being grateful for the gifts of creation. We tried to live more simply: hanging clothes on a line to dry, raising most of our own food, giving food to soup kitchens as much as possible, sharing farm equipment with neighbors, working collectively and making the land available for others to garden.

Our time on the farm was a delight, almost ten years of extremely hard but very satisfying work. We put deep roots into the foothills of the Appalachian mountains, seeing extreme poverty and injustice there that we had not dreamed was possible in the United States.

At the same time we made efforts to keep in view the "margins" of the world, where the poor and the earth are struggling to survive. Farm life in many ways was idyllic, and it was very demanding of our time. There was always good work to do. We could easily have turned inward completely. But we believed that to do so would have been to ignore the gospel call to "participate in the transformation of the world," as it was being so clearly articulated in those years following Vatican II. It seemed extremely important to keep our family's attention outward on a world that was broken as well as inward on our own lifestyle and the challenges of a small farm. So we answered another "call," looking for ways to stay involved in the work for social change — locally, nationally, and globally.

We tried to engage in the work for social justice and peace from where we were. To help make that possible, two friends and I founded the Center for New Creation, an ecumenical organization that worked for peace and social justice, promoting dialogue across difference about critical issues like the nuclear arms race, the repression and violence in Central America, and the right of impoverished people to a dignified life. I worked at the Center part time in the beginning, often involving the children in different projects like the Blue Ridge Peace Pilgrimage to heighten awareness of the dangers of nuclear war or the Peace Ribbon event on the fortieth anniversary of the atomic bombings in Hiroshima and Nagasaki.

Based on the creative idea of a woman from Denver, Colorado, named Justine Merritt, tens of thousands of people across the country and around the world stitched or painted or glued or otherwise created a representation of "what they could not bear to think of as lost in a nuclear war" on a piece of cloth three feet long by eighteen inches high. The Center for New Creation was asked to organize an event at the Pentagon when all the pieces of cloth would be held end-to-end to create a Peace Ribbon that we would "tie" around that center of U.S. military power. In the end we had twenty-six miles of ribbon when all the pieces were assembled and held end to end, enough to go around the Pentagon, across the Potomac River, all the way down the Mall, around the Capitol building, back up the other side of the Mall, around the Ellipse by the White House and back across the river to the Pentagon!

My husband became involved in an international program to raise awareness about poverty among medical and dental students in the United States. He began to accompany students to the Dominican Republic and Colombia. Occasionally, I went with him, as did each of our two oldest daughters.

A PAINFUL NEXT STEP

After nine years on the farm and almost twenty years of marriage, my husband left our family and I found myself single again — with six children between the ages of one and sixteen. In many ways it was like falling into a black hole. What was I being called to do now?

Slowly, a new direction began to come into focus. To stay on the farm would have been very difficult alone, especially as our older children were beginning to move into their own lives and activities and had less and less time for family farming. For me to farm as a single adult would have been completely consuming, precluding any involvement in the work for social justice and peace. So we moved to the small town near our parish and the children's schools and concentrated on regrouping and shoring each other up through a troubled time. But as we regained our balance, this new "call" began to take shape.

For the first time, as part of my work at the Center for New Creation, I had the opportunity to visit El Salvador and Guatemala, countries then at war. I learned about deep faith in the context of terrible violence, about human rights violations that took my breath away, about the importance of solidarity and the challenge of accompanying people in great danger when all I could offer was presence and love. I became increasingly aware of the remarkable international community of people who have given their lives to solidarity with the poor, whose vocations were shaped by their relationships with people living on the margins, struggling to survive and to live with dignity in dreadful conditions. I wanted to draw my family closer to this wonderful community and allow the depth of meaning and commitment I saw there to influence their young lives.

My oldest daughter was by then in college and more or less on her own. My oldest son, whose heart was in the country, had finished high school and was planning to live and work on a farm near where ours had been, at least for a year. The rest of us — one just starting college, two in high school, a five-year-old and I — took a leap of faith and moved into the Assisi Community as founding members.

INTO COMMUNITY

Assisi Community, according to our mission statement, is a small, intentional, Catholic Christian community of individuals and families, women and men, teenagers, children, professed religious and lay people who are striving to live faithfully the gospel call to work for a more just and peaceful world, who are trying to put into practice the values of Jesus, "living our way," so to speak, into the New Creation.

The mission statement continues,

> We are particularly touched by the tradition of Francis and Clare, by the base communities of Latin America, and by the charisms of religious communities whose members have joined us. We are striving to articulate a new spirituality informed by the joining of lay spirituality with that of religious. . . . We intentionally emphasize mutuality and participation and find that real dialogue about important community issues (as well as global issues) is a vital part of life. We make a conscious effort to be sensitive and enabling of each other. Decisions are made by consensus.

Members of Assisi Community live in two big old row houses in the inner city of Washington, DC, accessible to each other across a rather bleak alley. The community's common ground is an effort to "live simply" (a very basic, mostly meatless diet, frugal use of appliances and utilities, simple household furnishings, sharing of cars, etc.) and to support each other's commitment to and work for social justice and peace.

There are usually between twelve and eighteen people of all ages in the community. Some have stayed for many years (Assisi Community celebrated its twentieth anniversary in 2006), others for a year or two. Many other families have also joined the community. We moved into the community as soon as the children and I were ready, a few months after the first house was opened. A family of seven, refugees from the war in El Salvador, was already living at Assisi Community by then, although they had their own kitchen and a somewhat separate routine.

Since the beginning, Assisi Community has prayed together every morning, gone on retreat together twice a year, and celebrated Eucharist together two or three times a week, including on Monday nights, our community meeting night. Those who are home eat dinner together. Everyone takes turns cooking for the whole community, and other chores, such as food shopping and housecleaning, also are equally shared.

There is no single authority figure in the community. Different community members with particular experience or knowledge play leadership roles in different situations.

Expenses of the household are divided among wage-earners. For example, I paid one share for four children and myself, the same as a single person with an income would pay. Those were lean years for me financially and sharing household expenses with others kept the wolf away from our door.

Each single person in the community has his or her own room; families usually share two or three rooms. I think we had three and a half rooms when we first moved into Assisi. It was a huge change from a sixty-five-acre farm and a house of our own, but we gradually adjusted and figured out how to find family time in the midst of all the community activity. In spite of the fact that we lived with so many wonderful people, I believed that it was really important to maintain a clear sense of our own identity as a family. I wanted my youngest son, who was only five, to be clear about my role as his mother. Members of the community were wonderful in helping that to happen.

As mentioned, we lived in an inner city neighborhood of Washington, DC, sharing the dangers and hopes, fears and joys of a largely impoverished part of our nation's capital. My children grew in wisdom and benefited enormously from the gift of their experience in the neighborhood, and especially from the richness of their interaction with members of the community, whose own journeys and diverse vocations provided a remarkable set of role models for them. Even the two who never lived in the community — and the older ones who moved in and out as their own lives took shape — were deeply affected in a most positive way by Assisi Community.

My youngest son, who grew up in the community, now describes that experience as one of tremendous security; of awesome encounters with people who lived in or visited Assisi Community from all over the world (survivors of torture and war, Nobel laureates, authors, theologians, human rights activists, teachers committed to inner-city education, community organizers, social justice advocates, and activists).

He was enriched by his interaction with people from our neighborhood, especially the strong, wise grandmothers and the Catholic Workers. His memory, amazingly, is one of stability, in spite of the fact that I was traveling more, and of fun.

Living in the community was challenging. There was little physical space for family time, though we managed pretty well. It was also very intense. The reality of a broken world was on our doorstep all the time because the members of the community were right in the middle of the struggle for truth and social justice. But living in the community also was very, very good.

CALLED TO MARYKNOLL

Shortly after we moved into Assisi Community I had the good fortune of being given another "call": to work for Maryknoll, the U.S.-based Catholic missionary movement founded almost a hundred years ago and now present in thirty-nine countries around the world. Eventually I was named director of the Maryknoll Office for Global Concerns, a collaborative office of three different Maryknoll organizations: the Maryknoll Sisters, the Maryknoll Fathers and Brothers, and the Maryknoll Lay Missioners.

Our job is to bring the experience of Maryknoll missioners and of the mostly very poor communities where they live and work to the consciousness of people in the United States and especially into decision-making processes at the United Nations, the U.S. government, the World Bank, and the IMF — wherever policies are being developed and practices shaped that will have an impact on the poor and vulnerable, on the environment, and on possibilities for peace, especially in those places where Maryknollers serve. Our goals are clear but very long range: peace on earth, social justice, and ecological integrity. We try to educate the U.S. public and decision makers.

When we can, we go to countries in conflict to express solidarity with those who are most harmed by war. That was the point of my multiple visits to El Salvador during the years of violence and war there. That was the point of my journey with Pax Christi to Israel, Palestine, and Jordan at the end of the first Gulf War; to Pakistan and Afghanistan in June of 2002; to Colombia on several occasions.

We promote justice for (and often with) people who are particularly vulnerable in many parts of the world: women, children, people with HIV/AIDS, migrants, and indigenous people. To do so, we work very closely with Maryknoll missioners serving those populations, visiting the countries where they work, bringing them to speak, most often at the United Nations, but also to the U.S. public and officials in Washington, DC.

We work for economic justice. Maryknoll was one of the first organizations in the world to call for debt cancellation for impoverished countries. We promote justice in trade agreements, expressing to decision makers our opinion as shaped by the gospel and Catholic social teaching.

We pay close attention to U.S. foreign policy, pressing for a return of the "good neighbor approach" to international relations in this age of globalization. We promote a very different idea of security than that defined in U.S. national security documents. We work for human security, for a state of well-being with basic needs met and a life of dignity assured for all people everywhere.

And we promote within Maryknoll and beyond respect for the integrity of creation, for ecological wholeness. Almost all of our work requires a really long-term commitment. It is a vocation in itself. Work that we believe in often is. The heart of the matter is in the "doing" itself.

A CALL TO ACCOMPANIMENT

I was completely and happily ensconced in this work, living in and being challenged by Assisi Community and accompanying my children as they matured into their own vocations, when another "call" came around the corner, perhaps the most challenging of all and one increasingly heard in our aging society. It was a call to me as a daughter to take care of my mom as she approached ninety and was no longer able to live alone; she needed companionship if not much physical care at that time. As so often happens on life's journey, I had no idea how profoundly this new vocation would affect my own life. We found a little house to share that met our needs and moved in together. I no longer lived in the Assisi Community house, but as much as was possible, I remained a part of the community, returning each morning for prayers and each Monday evening for the community meeting. I continued to work for Maryknoll. But as my mom slowed down, my pace had to slow down as well. My life narrowed to work and family and the challenge of learning how to care for her pulled my soul in new directions and provoked a profound re-thinking of my values and priorities and expectations about life. I had to learn to let go and follow the Spirit into un-known places, much as I had when, twenty years earlier, I had found myself suddenly single again, and with overwhelming responsibilities. No call is given without the grace to respond. I suspect that more invitations will be issued as I move into my own senior years. My children now are all adults. Our family is expanding delightfully to include children-in-law and grandchildren. As they settle into their own lives, my understanding of "call" has grown even deeper and richer. Each of them has woven into the work they are doing, into the ways that they parent, into their relationships, into their lives as citizens, the values of and a deep commitment to the New Creation. As I observe their lives, their efforts to be faithful to "the good," whether they express that in the language of faith or not, I am struck by the richness of the journey through life and by the great diversity of vocations.

I invite you to contemplate your own experience, whether you are on the threshold of life or well into the fray. The reflections that follow flow obviously from my own journey. May they illuminate your own understanding of vocation as a blessed invitation from the Spirit of Life to mission in family, in community, in a hungry and hurting world.

Chapter One ———————————————————

Catching the Rhythm of God's Voice

Then one of the seraphs flew to me holding a live coal that had been taken from the altar with a pair of tongs. The seraph touched my mouth with it and said, "Now that this has touched your lips, your guilt has departed and your sin is blotted out." Then I heard the voice of the Lord saying, "Whom shall I send, and who will go for us?" And I said, "Here I am; send me!" (Isaiah 6:6–8)

He began to teach them many things in parables, and in his teaching he said to them, "Listen! A sower went out to sow. And as he sowed, some seed fell on the path, and the birds came and ate it up. Other seed fell on rocky ground, where it did not have much soil, and it sprang up quickly, since it had no depth of soil. And when the sun rose, it was scorched; and since it had no root, it withered away. Other seed fell among thorns, and the thorns grew up and choked it, and it yielded no grain. Other seed fell into good soil and brought forth grain, growing up and increasing and yielding thirty and sixty and a hundredfold." And he said, "Let anyone with ears to hear listen!" (Mark 4:2–9)

"THEN I HEARD the voice of the Lord.... Listen!" Catch the rhythm of God's voice. Sometimes we hear it deep in our own souls; at other times, through a dialogue of the heart with another person; or through discernment in community; or in something we read or observe about the earth herself or events in the world.

John Neafsey writes about the "divine source of wisdom, mysteriously both beyond and within ourselves" that "guides us in the path of our true calling and summons us to our destiny."[4]

To understand our vocation we need to listen to that "still, small voice" within us. God is whispering to us all the time about the good, the happiness to which we are called, but it is hard to hear God's voice because we are too distracted, too overwhelmed with internal and external noise. We need to be still, to lay aside concerns about money, security, and ambition, and catch the rhythm of God's voice. Then we will begin to discern our vocation, the kind of person we are called to be.

"Letting the land of our lives lie fallow," according to religious educator Maria Harris, who died after a long illness in 2005, is to allow "the tiny country each of us comprises, whose geography we know so well to rest." We are, she claimed, to let that land be still — "the land of our bodies, our blood, our breath, and our bones...giving it not only physical nourishment but regular, ritual rest."[5]

One characteristic of many societies in these early days of the twenty-first century, our own included, is a nearly frenetic level of activity. In impoverished countries and communities, this often is "survival" activity — work for little or no pay that provides (often barely) for the basic necessities of life. In wealthier settings busy-ness has many faces relating to both work and leisure. "Letting the land of our lives lie fallow" is a tremendous challenge to an economy that drains the last drop of energy out of workers trying to make ends meet; to cultures that define the value of persons by their job description, level of income, or possessions, and to lifestyles that fill every nook and cranny outside of work or school of every day with noise or electronic images or organized play.

Practicing Shabat

In the Judeo-Christian tradition, one antidote to this situation is shabat, the sabbatical, the jubilee. Abundance — the thirty-, sixty-, hundred-fold — is the fruit of stopping, setting limits. And stopping, setting limits, creating the space in our lives to "be," enables us to hear the rhythm of God's voice in our own souls, through dialogue with another, through discernment in community, in communion with nature. Stopping, setting limits, creating space in our lives sometimes makes it possible for us to see the reality of our world or the earth with new eyes, to imagine in new ways our own next steps.

For many of the past thirty years I have been involved in the work for social justice and peace. I have spent long, long days and seven-day weeks at work, loving what I was doing and, in fact, defining "faithfulness" by the number of hours I spent working each day, each week, each month. Between working and tending to my children and relating to Assisi Community, there was not much time for *listening*.

At one point along the way, something in my being became desperate for space, for physical space (of which there was not much in our community houses, where we were living at that time) and for soul space. I suspect most of us have reached that point at one time or another in our busy lives.

For a long time I sat with that yearning, trying to take a step in some direction toward what felt like necessary but utterly unreachable relief. Those steps I did try to take were often too big, too uncertain. I simply could not regularly take weekends off, or even Sundays. As soon as I said, "I will take every other Saturday off to re-create myself," or "I will never work on Sunday," something unavoidable came up. I couldn't find an evening that could be freed on a regular basis from a wide variety of obligations. I began to think about what I could realistically do that would weave my body and soul back together, and a few pieces began to make sense: time with my children and their children (especially as they approached adulthood our time together was never long enough or often enough, but it was always healing) — and dirt.

When we joined Assisi Community in 1987, we had moved from a very rural area where we had grown most of our own food into an inner-city neighborhood where cement covered almost every square foot of soil. I had tried and tried to grow anything in the small yard of the house in which we lived, but to no avail. No sunlight could find its way around our tall urban row house to shine on the little bit of dirt in its front yard. The longer, narrow backyard was almost all cement.

But that year, as I doggedly pursued wholeness, I found I had neglected to notice a very small patch of earth in front of one of our community houses. There I dug in compost and manure and planted and cared for a tiny, really tiny, little garden and found that what grew there was much, much more than beans and tomatoes and eggplant! Taking twenty minutes or half an hour, even at 5:00 a.m., to get my hands in the soil drew my attention to that place and helped me to live in that moment. And my little garden began to nurture my relationships with others living in our neighborhood as well. People I had never seen before stopped by to comment as the vegetables grew. Many had grown up on farms in North Carolina or Virginia. They wanted to know what kind of tomatoes I had planted and just how they were doing. The little harvest was a treat that went well beyond Assisi Community! And I began to feel more whole, more woven together, more integrated, better able to listen to the voice within and better able to converse, really converse with others.

I share this little story here not because it offers a formula, but as encouragement to listen to the stirrings of the Spirit in your own life, knowing for sure that She will guide you toward right pathways and wholeness. And perhaps even more to share with you a few of the lessons I gleaned from this simple Sabbath practice that has been so enormously enriching in my life:

- that in one way or another, we who are trying to catch the rhythm of God's voice and allow it to set the direction of our lives need to create spaces to be present and attentive, for the stirrings of the Spirit are often drowned out by our daily routines that are packed with even-very-good activities.

- that although the Sabbath might feel like a necessary nurturing time for our own survival, it is much, much more about righting relationships with others (our neighbors, our children, our friends, our communities, our enemies) than about anything turned too intensely inward. Sabbath invites us to live in a manner carefully attuned to the world in which we live, with all its hopes and fears, joys and sorrows. Unless we are still enough to see (really see) what is going on in our broken world, we will never have the will or capacity to accept a vocation that participates in its healing.

- that we cannot separate ourselves from the earth. In some manner Sabbath practice has to be about righting our relationship with the rest of creation and discerning vocation there. Growing something in the front yard was for me an entry point back into a deeper connection with the place I call home, an invitation to help heal the illness of "placelessness" that is afflicting our world. More and more we are uprooted people, able to participate in the pillaging of creation because we have no allegiance to and no roots sunk into a particular piece of home called earth.

- that Sabbath, even tiny Sabbath practice, is profoundly countercultural and even more counter to the prevailing wisdom of free market capitalism. It takes some real discipline and faith to believe that I am valuable, not because I am producing or consuming today, but because I *am*. To opt out of buying and selling even long enough to tend a tomato plant goes against the grain of a system that helps us create needs in a world where the real needs of a vast majority are never met; that tells us to buy more in a world of terrible waste; that tells us to produce

more, to exploit the rest of creation in any way necessary, to grow our economies without limit on a planet
with very real limits that are rapidly approaching!

Sabbath practice, if it is genuine, will lead us to participate
in the transformation of the world, the gospel vocation described so clearly by the Synod of Bishops in 1971: "It fully
appears to us," they said, "that action for justice and participation in the transformation of the world are constitutive to
the preaching of the Gospel."[6] "We need," continues Maria
Harris,

> to be people whose every activity has an underlying
> residue of receptivity, quiet and contemplative being.
> We need to be listeners: not only to the creation sur-
> rounding us, but to the creation and the land that
> we are.... Sabbath means that we live in time, in the
> present. Sabbath means that we practice shavat.... It
> means that we stop.[7]

But *where* we are when we stop will also affect our ability
to catch the cadence of God's voice. Here two of the lessons
from my own tiny Sabbath practice may be worth rewriting:

1. Sabbath is about righting relationships, living in a
   manner carefully attuned to the world in which we live,
   from near to far, with all its hopes and fears, joys and
   sorrows. Unless we are still enough to see (really see)
   what is going on around us, we will never have the will
   or capacity to accept a vocation that participates in its
   (and thereby our own) healing.

2. We cannot separate ourselves from the earth. In some
manner Sabbath practice also has to be about righting
our relationship with the rest of creation and discerning
vocation there.

God's Voice in Friendship

For many of us, discerning vocation is about establishing
or nurturing right relationships — within and around our
families and places of work, our parishes and community activities, our blocks or towns or neighborhoods. If we listen,
we can hear the rhythm of God's call close to home.

Several years ago, in *St. Francis and the Foolishness of
God*, I, with several other authors, wrote a whole chapter
on friendship — as a source of renewal and joy, a source of
courage, a source of revolutionary accompaniment, a place
of accountability, and a place to meet God.[8]

True friendship, we said, "nourishes our capacity to move
through suffering.... [It] is a place where grief is made bear-
able and where we find the strength to even face death."[9] True
friendship "fills us with a desire for the good."[10]

"Our deepest friendships offer us the possibility of confronting in ourselves the inclinations to stray from the journey toward New Creation.... Truly loving and respectful
confrontation toward genuine accountability in Christian
discipleship is most possible in the safe place of intimate
relationships."[11]

We wrote about the important links between life in God
and life in another. "Life in God, for example, requires an
other-centeredness not unlike selfless friendship.... Life in

God requires that we risk all in the cosmic effort to live justly. Intimacy requires that we risk as well — in the miraculous discovery of mutually respectful, life-giving, and just relationships."[12]

The role of friendship in the discernment of vocation is key. In fact, friendship itself may be a vocation that contributes generously to discerning the will of God in our lives — at any age. What could that mean? What would such a vocation look like? What would it mean to say yes to *this* vocation?

For as long as I can remember, my life has been overloaded. I have always said yes to much more than I could possibly manage and have constantly scrambled from one end of the day to the other. I have a wonderfully loving family, who are among my dearest friends, and I have cherished friends, all of whom have forgiven me over and over for being so hard to pin down.

Either I don't have, or I have never acknowledged, a personal vocation to friendship. Yet I have witnessed and been beneficiary of the friendship of others who have clearly embraced this vocation and allowed it to help shape who they are and how they are present in the world.

One dear friend, now retired, is the matriarch of a very large family. She provides hospitality, transportation, an open heart, a listening ear, nursing care, a challenging conversation, honest advice, childcare, a good argument, a game of tennis, a family recipe, prayer, wisdom, encouragement, and unrelenting friendship to the most amazing spectrum of people — from children and grandchildren to strangers, from friends in or retired from the Navy to those protesting U.S. foreign policy, from the very wealthy to the very poor. Over and over again, her wisdom and attention have helped people catch the rhythm of God's voice. Her vocation to friendship has been well tended for over a decade.

Another dear friend, a Franciscan brother who lived in Assisi Community for many years, also has a vocation to friendship. His cup of tea and handwritten, snail-mail notes in an e-mail age are characteristic of his whole approach to life. His Franciscan vocation has enabled him to nurture friendship in some of our country's most forsaken places — in the parishes of poor neighborhoods, in soup kitchens, in prisons, in an AIDS hospice. He stays in contact with my children, visited them when they were away at school, and remembers their special days. He does the same with all the children of Assisi Community — and so many other friends. They have caught the rhythm of God's voice through his friendship, through his vocation to friendship, which also has been well tended.

God's Voice at the Margins

Right relationships at a personal level are vitally important. Right relationships with people who are impoverished and excluded are equally important for all of us.

The Sabbath practice of righting relationships in a world where poverty and brokenness abound may help move us in that direction. Neafsey reminds us that we will hear the Voice of God "by listening with an open heart to the cry of the poor and the oppressed."[13] In other words, our vocational possibilities will be clearer if we look for them through the lived experience of those in our world who are excluded from the benefits of society and by more frequent encounters with the painful reality of a threatened earth.

One of the most powerful and disturbing experiences of my own life was realizing that I could neither see nor hear the word of God as long as our family's life was isolated from the broken reality that shaped the experience of the majority of people in the world. The long, long journey toward a simpler lifestyle with more direct connections to people living on the margins in our own country and around the world is very far from over for me. I suspect it never will be.

The steps we have taken — especially from suburbia to an organic farm, where we could experience the kind of work for survival and right relationship with the rest of creation that shape the lives of so many of the world's poor; and from the farm to Assisi Community, where inner-city poverty and violence were woven into the fabric of our lives — were vital, but I know there will be many more steps necessary in the future. Over and over again, we who come from an affluent world have to reappropriate our vocation of relinquishment and relocate ourselves in relationship to the poor. On the way, I believe, the rhythm of God's call will become more clear.

In *St. Francis and the Foolishness of God*, we wrote,

> the gospel calls us to the margins of society in order to bring about the conversion that is begun in our encounter with the poor. . . . Relinquishment is much more than giving up material goods. It means giving up prestige and privilege, learning to listen and to accept criticism and learning how to use our power differently and ultimately to share . . . the power available to us —

our resources of wealth, education, influence and access — with those who lack these things.... The way
of relinquishment is the lifelong process of removing
the obstacles to loving and just relationships with our
neighbors on this earth.[14]

The way of relinquishment opens space in our lives to hear
the call of our God, to discern the movement of the Spirit in
our lives.

Seeing Reality with New Eyes

One place of intersection between the poor and marginalized
of the world and affluent and powerful people of faith who
lived in the suburbs of Washington, DC, was the Center for
New Creation, where an important dimension of my own
vocation was nurtured and directed for over a decade.

In 1979 we wrote:

The Center for New Creation is a gathering of men and
women motivated by the Gospel to work together for a
just and peaceful society — who are striving to "let go"
of whatever they hold in excess of need so as to be in
solidarity with the poor as they reach out to take what
is rightfully theirs; whose mission is to seek initiatives,
both public and private, that would be a sign of that personal and societal relinquishment which promotes the
New Creation.

A few years later, we added:

We try to be an agency for social change, a voice that begins to connect our own personal and local experience of injustice with a broader, even global trend, ... a voice that enables us to see the far-reaching effect of lives lived here, of choices made here, ... a community whose primary reason for existence is to facilitate social transformation towards a just society.

An important goal of Center programs was to orchestrate encounters between the two vastly different worlds of poor and nonpoor and thereby to create a context in which the privileged, ourselves included, could catch the rhythm of God's call.

One of the most powerful and disturbing experiences of my own life was realizing that I could neither see nor hear the word of God as long as our family's life was isolated from the broken reality that shaped the experience of the majority of people in the world.

Regularly, we brought people from the margins of our world in El Salvador or Honduras or Appalachia to tell their stories in affluent, powerful northern Virginia. We published their stories and perspectives in *New Creation News*. We brought delegations from wealthy U.S. parishes to El Salvador, Guatemala, and Nicaragua. We brought people from the suburbs into Washington, DC, neighborhoods that were both broken and full of life, where they had previously never ventured.

Slowly, slowly all of us began to get a glimmer of what life was like at the margins. We saw devastating poverty, the horrific impact of war on human life, and the frustration of people for whom the "system" was a source of oppression. But we also saw incredible hope, determination, and faith. In those years, base communities in Central and South America with which we were interacting both here and there were bringing the gospel to life in their own communities and countries in amazing ways — in spite of, or perhaps because of, terrible violence and repression. Over and over again we were led by their faith to ask what we, as middle-class people of faith in the United States, should be doing in response to the struggles for social justice, peace, and dignity of our brothers and sisters around the world. We were led by them to listen with great care to the movement of the Spirit in our lives and our communities, to try to catch the rhythm of God's particular call to us in those years.

Maryknoll at the Margins

That challenge continued for me when I began to work for Maryknoll. One of the great gifts of accompanying Maryknoll missioners has been in the consequent relocation of my own life's journey.

Maryknollers are present in almost forty countries, in the slums and barrios of growing urban centers, in rural villages, in refugee camps, in indigenous communities, among women and people sick with HIV/AIDS and with people on the move. Always there they find, and help me find, life and hope. Always there they hear, and help me hear, the call, the vocation to discipleship, the invitation to follow Jesus.

In Oaxaca, for example, Maryknoll lay missioners have witnessed the struggle of Mayan farmers to survive as the agricultural reality of Mexico shifted from *ejido* production for local consumption to large-scale exportation of specialty crops.

In East Africa, Southeast Asia, and Central America, Maryknoll missioners see the utter devastation of HIV/AIDS and other treatable diseases.

In Panama, South Korea, Puerto Rico, and the Philippines, Maryknoll missioners have lived with the social and environmental consequences of a huge U.S. military presence.

In Kenya they watched a people struggle to oust a tyrant and reclaim their own system from rampant corruption.

In Tanzania and Nicaragua they lived through hope-filled times when the New Creation seemed just around the corner. Tanzanian president Julius Nyerere, who is now a candidate for canonization, was a parishioner and friend of Maryknoll missioners in Tanzania. The foreign minister of Nicaragua after the revolution that threw out dictator Anastasio Somoza was a Maryknoll priest. Maryknollers lived through the devastation of those dreams and the repeated impoverishment of the people they loved, and they saw glimmers of hope again on the horizon from time to time.

In Chile and Brazil, lay missioners and sisters accompany women resisting violence and reclaiming self-esteem. In Honduras, Zimbabwe, and Cambodia they do the same with youth and children.

In the Sudan and East Timor, in the Great Lakes region in Africa, in Palestine and Guatemala they have experienced first hand the impact of what seemed like unending war and violence.

On the U.S.-Mexican border and the Burmaese-Thai border they have seen the frustration of millions of people trying to cross a dangerous border to make ends meet day after day.

In the Philippines, Panama, Mexico, Tanzania, Chile, and Zimbabwe they accompany the earth and feel her pain. In Bolivia, East Africa, Bangladesh, Panama, and Nepal they live with the immediate impact of global warming.

The long, long journey toward a simpler lifestyle with more direct connections to people living on the margins in our own country and around the world is very far from over for me. I suspect it never will be.

As I visited them in many of these places and began to look at the world through an even broader lens, I found the challenge constant and heard the question asked over and over again: What am I called to do to be a faithful follower of Jesus in these times in this world? Who and how am I called to be in this broken world?

To see reality through the eyes of those who are now excluded and impoverished is a vital step toward vocational discernment. In some ways this might seem antithetical to the kind of sabbath living I described above, but I don't believe it is. We have to learn to listen to the "inner voice," but we also have to find ways to do so that are deeply rooted in the margins of our world where the rhythm of God's call is most clear.

Listening in Community

Every human being is unique and uniquely beloved by our Creator God. In many ways we are profoundly alone as we discern the meaning and shape of vocation in our own lives, as we listen for "my" call to discipleship. But human beings are also persons in community, and that fact will affect our hearing.

Although the Assisi Community has been central to my journey for many years, several other communities have been important in my life, making me acutely aware that communities come in all shapes and sizes.

Pilgrims after Christ

One community that was extremely important in my own formation process was the Pax Community, a Eucharistic community in northern Virginia that has celebrated Mass together every Sunday since 1969. Founded within a parish in the years immediately following the Second Vatican Council, Pax ("Pilgrims After Christ") has been committed from the beginning to excellent liturgical preparation, to actively supporting and challenging each other to live the gospel, and to service in the wider community.

Every week a team of Pax members meets with the priest who will celebrate the Eucharist on the following Sunday to identify and develop a theme based on the readings.

The careful exegesis and rich reflections they share result in meaningful homilies, prayers, and music and help the whole community deepen its ability to hear the word of God.

As the community matured, a deep concern for social justice led to thoughtful discussions, sometimes across significant differences of opinion, and to action.

I remember in the early years, when Pax was discerning its mission, reading with others in the community a little pamphlet by Elizabeth O'Connor from the Church of the Saviour in Washington, DC. Entitled *Calling Forth of Charisma,* it was the impetus for many Pax Community conversations about vocation and mission that shaped my own sense of "call" and, many years later, affected the way I responded to my children as they discerned directions in life.

In the Pax Community early on I also witnessed a very deep generosity of spirit, time, and treasure that enabled the community to provide extensive daily support for a dying member of the community, a witness that has been repeated many times in the thirty-five plus years of the Pax Community's existence and that shaped my own understanding of vocation in communal terms. I believed then that I was called to be a wife and mother, a homemaker, and to be occasionally involved in community service work, but I also began to see that a deep and real commitment to community life, with all its gifts and demands and challenges, was to be an essential part of my own and our family's vocation.

Listening Together at the Center for New Creation

Another, smaller community that was very important in my own life was the community that gathered around the

Center for New Creation. There, *process* was key: the way we worked together was intentionally shaped by what we claimed to believe. All major decisions were made in a participatory manner, and we worked very hard to promote real dialogue, even across significant differences of opinion. The positions we took on the critical social justice and peace issues of the 1980s were shaped by consensus and rooted as much as possible in the experience of the people we were coming to know who lived on the margins of the world; in careful analysis to identify root causes of poverty, war, and oppression; and in the gospel and Catholic social teaching. Over ten years of experiencing what was a really wonderful model of shared discernment also made me shy about trying to hear God's call on my own, which gave strong impetus to my decision to help found and make a long-term commitment to Assisi Community.

Listening with Assisi Community

Assisi Community has had an extremely important and positive influence on my understanding of vocation as well. The diversity of age and deep life experience of community members provides a unique base for shared discernment. Our commitment to daily prayer and reflection on the signs of the times, plus weekly community meetings and twice-yearly retreats, affords ample opportunity to develop the habit of careful listening and fruitful dialogue when important decisions are to be made by individual members of Assisi Community or by the community as a whole.

Often in Assisi Community we are able to encourage each other to hear the invitations of the Spirit we might prefer to

ignore and to take steps that are risky or exceptionally difficult. Without the community's support, I suspect that many of
us would simply ignore the still, small voice that John Neafsey
describes so well. Neafsey writes, "The image of the still,
small voice resonates deeply with many people. It seems to
capture something of the depth and nuance and mystery of
the inner voice, the patience and practice it takes to hear it,
and our intuition that there really is something *worth* listening for beneath all the noise and activity on the surface of our
lives."[15]

In 1992, as the quincentenary of Columbus's arrival in the
Americas approached, many people where suggesting that
the time was appropriate for a deep apology to the indigenous peoples whose ancient roots went very deep in this land
and whose numbers were decimated by violence and disease
after the Europeans arrived. Public and private events were
planned across the Americas to hear the story retold from the
perspective of native peoples and to ask for their forgiveness.

With a focus on Latin America in my work for Maryknoll,
I had visited many of the countries in the Americas and knew
well the devastating story of the indigenous peoples. I was
acutely aware of the significance of the quincentenary for
many indigenous groups and was listening very carefully for
movement of the Spirit in terms of how to respond. When I
received an invitation to participate in a forty-two-day water-
only fast, I knew my answer had to be yes. But I am not sure
I would have even heard the invitation and I know I would
not have considered it a possibility for me had I not lived in
and prayed with Assisi Community at the time. In explaining
the reasons for my fast, I wrote in part:

We are called to make concrete and visible the signs of our repentance and to offer them in all humility to the ones who have suffered from our unjust ways. We are called to risk all in the cosmic effort to live justly. We are called to shape our journeys in a manner explicitly informed by the Gospel we proclaim. We are called to resist evil, but to go beyond resistance into life "as if," and to believe that in the process of profound conversion we will discover who we are, who are our brothers and sisters, how we are to live with all of creation, and toward what vision of life we are to journey together.

Much could be said about the impact of that fast to which I felt a clear call. It was a difficult time for Assisi Community, for my family and co-workers and for me. Assisi Community helped keep it all in perspective, for I was neither the first nor the last member of the community to fast. It also was a graced time, a time of joy and deep meaning. My first grandchild was born on the eleventh day of the fast and I turned fifty two days later. Fasting focused my attention on both of those very significant events in my life, especially on my granddaughter's arrival, and cast them in a historical and a global context. My new vocation as grandmother would have to be infused with my consciousness of our society's great need for repentance and conversion. And I knew that the call to discipleship would be as demanding in my later years as it was early on.

There were many other times when Assisi Community provided fertile ground for catching the rhythm of God's voice. The presence and participation of community members whose own journeys began in situations of *in*voluntary poverty completely changed our conversations about voluntary poverty and simple lifestyles. Dehumanizing poverty could never be described as an ideal; only the kind of gospel (evangelical) poverty that helped close the gap between the rich and the poor was a state to which we might aspire.

The presence in the community of people from countries where the innocent disappeared at the hands of repressive governments challenged our discernment about civil disobedience with its *pro forma* few hours in jail.

The presence in the community of survivors of torture and war pushed us to listen more carefully to promptings of the Spirit with social and political consequences.

The presence in the community of survivors of childhood abuse made us place great value on the vocation of accompaniment within our own community.

The support of Assisi Community actually made it possible for me to live simultaneously my vocation to motherhood, by then as a single parent, and my vocation to the work for social justice and peace through Maryknoll, which included a lot of traveling.

The solid values of Assisi Community helped me hear as well the invitation to accompany my own mother in the last years of her life. My move out of Assisi Community to live with her was supported by the vision Assisi shared of community life embracing young and old and providing mutual support for each other at every stage of life. How to make care for the elderly and those with special needs possible in the context of community is an important question that remains before us.

An equally important role in the discernment process has been played by my family community, especially as my children have moved into adulthood. Their discernment was essential, for example, as I tried to figure out how to be a single mom or as we contemplated moving into Assisi Community and even more so, years later, as I, with their strong support as well, moved out of Assisi Community and struggled to fulfill the demanding vocation of caretaker for my aging mom.

Often I think in terms of our *family's* vocation, one rooted in the amazing experiences we've had together and shaped by the now often separate journeys of each one. Alone, as several different nuclear families, and as a vibrant and deeply interconnected extended family, what does vocation mean? How will *this* community respond to our "call"? Are we listening to the rhythm of God's call? What can we offer to the world together?

Listening with the Rest of Creation

Just as we are called to place ourselves on the margins of society and allow right relationships with those who live there to open our hearts to the divine invitation, so we are called to reshape our relationships with the rest of creation and to allow those new relationships to move us beyond where we are into a new way of life.

As the New Creation comes into being, we must be as present as possible to its unfolding; we must look for its signs and wonders and hear its groaning.... Created in the image of God, humanity's vocation is to participate fully with God in the process of creating a world where peace and justice reign, and to claim the divine image within us so that we can find our right relationship to creation.[16]

The groaning of creation in our times is in tune with the rhythm of God's call. Our vocation "to participate fully with God" in the creation/re-creation process will become more evident to us if our hearts and minds are attentive to life in all its wondrous forms around us. Listening to the cry of the earth sharpens our capacity to hear God's voice.

> *The challenge and opportunity before all of us is to choose carefully where we plant our feet while listening for the rhythm of God's call.*

When thirty years ago we responded to a call we thought we heard from the poor of the world and moved from a suburban neighborhood to a sixty-five-acre run-down farm, I was excited because we were trying to simplify our family's life. We were leaving behind many of our "more expensive" or unnecessary possessions, our "excess baggage." We were moving from comfort and convenience to discomfort and hard work. We were moving our children to a less advantaged school district, but one where a wonderful diversity of children and experiences awaited them. We were moving to a place where we would have the basics, we thought, but not much more. We were trying to "live simply so others could simply live." As we moved, we wrote to our neighbors that we had been very happy in the wonderful neighborhood where our family's life was centered, but that we had to try to put into practice what we claimed to believe: that none of us should have more than we need when others were struggling just to survive.

I had no idea how profoundly our lives would be affected by the years we spent on that farm and the deep relationship we would build with the earth there. We learned to farm organically, slowly retrieving the land from years of being dowsed with chemicals. We worked our fields and planted our gardens with old, low-tech equipment and lots of hand and back labor. We came to know every square foot of our sixty-five acres, where the rocks were, where the good soil was, where the ground tended to be too wet or too dry. In the summer and fall we handled every bale of hay and every tomato or bean or eggplant personally. Collectively, we knew every weed in the garden. As we introduced animals to the farm, we watched them settle into a good relationship with the land and with us as well. Every morning in the dark I listened to God's voice as I milked our cow.

We were outraged when low-flying planes spraying chemicals on nearby farms came too close to ours. I remember clearly our children on the roof of our little farmhouse shouting at the threatening plane to go away.

Our years of farming tied my soul to the land and the gently rolling mountains of western Virginia. When I head out west from Washington, DC, to visit my children who still live in rural Virginia, I am convinced over and over again that out there I can catch much more easily the rhythm of God's call. And even when I am not in the Virginia countryside, I can feel

God's presence in the city's beautiful trees, in my backyard garden, in the birds returning in the spring. At least from time to time, I find I have to listen for God's call with the rest of creation.

The challenge and opportunity before all of us is to choose carefully where we plant our feet while listening for the rhythm of God's call. Vocation, obviously, is lived in a wide variety of ways; there are many different pathways even in one faithful life, but the first step is a challenging one: to create the space in our lives to listen and to place ourselves in those situations where we can hear. By stopping to let the land of our lives lie fallow, by nurturing friendships, by moving to the margins, by ensconcing ourselves in communities committed to faithful discipleship, by living in harmony with the rest of creation, perhaps, just perhaps, we will catch the cadence of God's voice and hear the call or calls that are ours.

Chapter Two _____

Vocation to Discipleship

As Jesus passed along the Sea of Galilee, he saw Simon and his brother Andrew casting a net into the sea — for they were fishermen. And Jesus said to them, "Follow me and I will make you fish for people." And immediately they left their nets and followed him. As he went a little farther, he saw James, Son of Zebedee, and his brother John, who were in their boat mending the nets. Immediately, he called them; and they left their father Zebedee in the boat with the hired men, and followed him. (Mark 1:16–20)

Jesus went out again beside the sea. The whole crowd gathered around him and they taught him. As he was walking along he saw Levi, son of Alphaeus, sitting at the tax booth, and he said to him, "Follow me." And he got up and followed him. (Mark 2:13–14)

OVER TWENTY-FIVE YEARS AGO a young woman not long out of college stepped out of a promising corporate career into an extraordinary community of people immersed in life and struggling to defend themselves and their loved ones against violent death. Jean Donovan, a lay missioner and

51

member of the Cleveland Mission Team, made a fundamental option for the poor, for community, and for solidarity. She chose to accompany poor people of El Salvador in dangerous times, and on December 2, 1980, she was brutally murdered, martyred, with two Maryknoll sisters, Maura Clarke and Ita Ford, and Dorothy Kazel, an Ursuline sister, also from Cleveland.

In many ways Jean's life was not unique. She was young, well-educated, privileged, and on the brink of life. The love of life and energy that defined her character shaped her way of being in El Salvador as well. In the midst of the violence there she found deep meaning, important relationships, joy.

Two weeks before she was murdered, she wrote to a friend in Connecticut: "Several times I have decided to leave El Salvador. I almost could except for the children, the poor bruised victims of this insanity. Who would care for them? Whose heart would be so staunch as to favor the reasonable thing in a sea of their tears and helplessness. Not mine, dear friend, not mine."[17]

Jean opened herself to the vocation of accompaniment, not an easy vocation for a "can do" North American to accept. "Am I willing to suffer with the people here, the powerless?" asked her friend Ita Ford. "Can I say to my neighbors, 'I have no solutions to this situation; I don't know the answers, but I will walk with you, search with you, be with you.' "[18] What was extraordinary about Jean Donovan's vocation was not only that she was martyred for her commitment to a God of love and life, but that she *lived* that commitment with every fiber of her being. Christian vocation is a call to the fullness of life.

In the first set of invitations to discipleship that are woven into the Gospel of Mark (1:16–20 and 2:13–14), Jesus, according to biblical scholar Ched Myers, requires of those who would follow him not to leave the world, but to embark on a fundamental reordering of relationships, to help create an "alternative social order."

The call of Jesus is "absolute, disrupting the lives of potential recruits, promising them only a 'school' from which there is no graduation." Their world is coming to an end. "The kingdom has dawned, and it is identified with the discipleship adventure."[19]

The Discipleship Adventure

Turning toward life, toward the good, toward God is the first step in responding to one's vocation. It is the ground, the foundation, upon which the finer "details" are built. Choosing to live in a way that promotes human dignity and nurtures all life, honors truth, fosters right relationships with God, ourselves, the rest of the human community, and all of creation — and nurtures peace in our hearts, our homes, our neighborhoods, our nation, and our world — is not unique to people of faith, nor is it the monopoly of the followers of Christ. But Jesus' explicit call, "Come, follow me," imbues "vocation" with special meaning for us. Our yes is the most consistent, sure, and clear indication that next steps on the journey of life will be open to the grace and the movement of the Spirit.

Moral theology books speak about "fundamental option" as "a moral agent's use of his or her most basic freedom to choose how he or she will stand before God."[20] Theologian Josef Fuchs, S.J., writes about the working of grace that makes a person respond in "loving self-surrender to the love of God."[21]

The "absolute" call of Jesus will, or should, affect every nook and cranny of our lives: our spirituality and moral values, what we care about, how we use our time and resources, our relationships, our work. Neafsey writes,

> Vocation potentially touches and encompasses *every* level and dimension of our lives. This includes our family life, our love life, our creative interests and pursuits, and our politics. Basically, anything we do with our time and talents and resources can be infused with a sense of vocation. Callings can also be experienced in relation to any or all of the multiple roles in which we find ourselves at any given time.... It is also possible to experience different callings at different times of our lives, or to experience multiple callings at any particular time of our life.[22]

We may have created Sabbath space in our lives, moved to the margins, embraced friendship and community, and ventured into relationship with the rest of creation to better hear the call. How we respond is the next crucial question.

> I appeal to you, therefore, brothers and sisters.... Do not be conformed to this world, but be transformed by the renewing of your minds, so that you may discern what is the will of God — what is good and acceptable and perfect.

...as in one body we have many members, and not all the members have the same function; so we who are many are one body in Christ, and individually we are members, one of another. We have gifts that differ according to the grace given to us: prophecy, in proportion to faith; ministry, in ministering; the teacher, in teaching; the exhorter, in exhortation; the giver, in generosity; the leader, in diligence; the compassionate, in cheerfulness. (Rom. 12:1–8)

Jean Donovan simply said yes to an invitation she clearly heard through a dialogue of the heart with the poor of El Salvador, and forever after that she looked at life through a lens held by these poor communities at the margins of Salvadoran society.

Jean chose life. She said yes to an invitation she sometimes strained to hear, and her understanding of that call was honed slowly over time. She made a fundamental option to follow Simon and Andrew, James and John, Levi and all the other women and men who have followed Jesus. And "on the road" she began to understand better the heart of Jesus' message for her.

We all bring to our vocations our experiences, gifts, and relationships. We bring the obstacles and distractions that clutter our lives. We bring who we are and who we are willing to become. We bring the context in which we live and a particular time in history. And *we have gifts that differ according to the grace given to us.*

Vocation is not *only* about a "state in life," whether we are single or married or vowed in religious life, although it *is* about that. But vocation also is about the *totality* of how we live the gospel in these times in whatever state in life we choose or find ourselves.

Each one of us stands radically alone before God, accountable for our own lives and decisions. We are also persons in community — the human community, the earth community — embracing life as one with the many. Some of us remain single as adults, for a while or for life. Others are married, committed forever to sharing the journey with a particular partner. Some make vows in a religious community with a defined charism that will guide and shape their futures. Others make marriage vows: two free, distinct human beings who choose to weave their lives together.

We may have created Sabbath space in our lives, moved to the margins, embraced friendship and community, and ventured into relationship with the rest of creation to better hear the call. How we respond is the next crucial question.

All are alone; all are in community; all are called to be subjects of our own lives and to make the world a better place. Yet we are called in different ways.

Vocation to Single Life Not Alone

Too often, I think, we fail to honor the discipleship call to remain single and lay. Yet it is the lasting vocation of some of the most inspiring members of the human community and the vocation of many others for long periods in their lives. Single women and men who embrace fully their role as participants in the community of life can often bring the excellent gifts of self-esteem and personal integration to the relationships they form and a tremendous dedication and attention to the work that they do.

The life of Dorothy Day is an interesting example. We don't often think of her vocation as a model for the single life, but surely it was.

With her friend Peter Maurin, Dorothy Day founded the Catholic Worker movement. She did so as a single mother, raising her daughter, Tamar, with all the challenges and uncertainties that accompany that particular form of the single vocation. When I was learning to make important decisions for our family as a newly single parent, I remember being particularly inspired by Dorothy's apparent ability to incorporate Tamar into her own vocation with the Catholic Worker movement and to simultaneously sustain their vitally important mother-daughter relationship. Hers was a centeredness, an other-centeredness, often (though not uniquely) characteristic of people called to life as a single lay person. She was a "mother, sister, companion; worker, journalist, inspiration; radical activist and prophet. She relentlessly pursued the roots of injustice and violence and confronted the powerful in church and state to do the same. She walked on picket lines and went to jail as a result. Dorothy Day loved deeply and personally; she saw the world through the eyes of those who were poor because she lived in community with them.

By their measure she measured her own faithfulness and that of the society in which she lived."[23]

Dorothy Day was an extraordinary single lay woman. Other examples abound, in every community and every field of endeavor. One friend, who has given his life to living simply in community, uses his training in organizational development to support nonprofit groups doing excellent work in local communities; another spent years working for refugees and impoverished communities in El Salvador and Honduras; a third, through his work in the field of financial aid, made a prestigious university accessible to thousands of young people from the poorest neighborhoods of New York.

Priesthood and Religious Life

Once understood as the highest call, a vocation to religious life or to ordination remains an invitation to a life imbued with deep meaning and great dignity. I cannot write about that "call" except as an observer whose own journey has so often intersected with the lives of religious sisters and brothers and priests who live with tremendous integrity.

One of the truly great gifts of my work for Maryknoll and my life in Assisi Community has been to know well hundreds of faithful women and men religious and priests. They are not the only ones I know who have lived or tried to live the gospel, but they have done very well in the context of lifestyles that are in striking contrast to what is considered the ideal or the norm, at least in the United States. I have frequently observed their very deep commitment to the other, often a stranger, and to keeping their centers of gravity outside of themselves.

Assisi Community from the beginning in 1986 has always included one or two women and men religious — a Franciscan brother, a Franciscan priest, a sister of Loretto, a Precious Blood sister, an Ursuline sister, a School Sister of Notre Dame, a Columban priest. Each brought their own experience and the charism of their own religious institute to Assisi Community. Their lives were, without exception, vibrant examples of religious vocations lived faithfully. The call to poverty, obedience, and celibate chastity that they heard and answered was not a call *out* of life but a call *into* the nurturing of individual lives, especially the most abandoned and needy, and those in communities all around them.

Some of the long-term members of Assisi Community reflected on their own vocations to religious life:

A Franciscan brother: For me the Rule of Francis is to live the gospel, to be a little brother, to be at the service of others. I have been especially influenced by Matthew 25 and by Luke's story of Lazarus and the rich man, who didn't see Lazarus as a brother. I believe that Jesus came as our brother, not as a king, a prince, or a high priest. He came to serve and to be the suffering servant. Francis wanted to be like Jesus. I want to be a brother like them both.

A Franciscan priest: While I entered the Franciscans principally to become a priest, taking public vows as a member of that religious order made a deep and permanent impression on me. I came to understand that my fundamental commitment came not so much from priestly ordination but from my solemn promise to live the life that St. Francis of Assisi had designed for all who would become his brothers. Put another way, I came to think of myself as a friar minor who happened to be a priest and not the other way around.

This conviction came quite early in my lifelong journey as a Franciscan and sustained me through the times when I was tempted to back away from the life I had vowed and take another path. Many of our companions in the order made that choice, especially during the tumultuous years following the Second Vatican Council. For me, the fact that I had quite consciously and with full knowledge vowed to God that I would walk the way of St. Francis for my whole life proved crucial for me in those inevitable moments of doubt, disillusion, or weakness.

Placing the Franciscan vocation ahead of or more basic to my priestly call informed everything I came to do as an ordained minister. There is an intangible something that religious who are priests bring to ministry. Perhaps it is life as equals in community, or the support that one's brothers provide, or a less hierarchical view of priesthood.

An example may underscore my point. Not many months ago I stood in front of our Franciscan church and friary in midtown New York City talking with one of our well-known friar theologians. A street person came along with her bags of belongings and telltale ruddy complexion from too many nights exposed to the cold. My Franciscan brother saw her approach and with total ease greeted the woman by name and asked her something about her health. I was enormously impressed by that encounter, happy to see that this learned priest was first and foremost a Franciscan, brother to the downcast and needy. Two conclusions:

First, it goes without saying that God puts signposts all along our life's journeys. In my case the opportunity to live and work in Latin America after priestly ordination and the up-close look I had at dehumanizing poverty during those years; my order's decision to assign me as founding pastor of an upper-middle-class parish in Lima, Peru; first-hand contacts with liberation theology; and the Latin American Catholic Church's historic conversion to a "preferential option for the poor" following the Second Vatican Council—all made an enormous impact in guiding me as a human being, a Christian Catholic, and a Franciscan priest.

After returning to the United States, I encountered several communities of people who understood the need to question our country's responsibility for much of the poverty I had seen in Latin America. Members of those groups pointed me toward relevant pastoral and human rights work here in our country.

Second, as I look back now on more than seven decades of life, it's clear that I came to recognize the signposts that God placed along my way mainly through hindsight. My guess is that it's the same for most people. As I passed them, I did not recognize those indicators as the hand of God leading me where Love wished me to go. As a result I've come to understand that while vocation discernment surely requires thought and prayer on our part, in the end it pretty much comes down to placing ourselves in God's hands.

A Sister of the Precious Blood: The values of my parents were very important in the shaping of my own vocation to religious life. They encouraged me to explore my desire for a life of service with the people of God. They nurtured my desire to join a group of women I admired, who were doing good work and living good lives, a group that was bigger than myself.

Although we entered religious life with a sense of the importance of community, I think we grew into the possibilities of this commitment after we entered the convent and the community itself grew and changed over time as it tried to integrate different understandings of the role of religious communities in the church and the world.

The charism of our community was very much influenced by the older sisters from Germany, whose strong sense of peace and the love of God helped shape the spirituality of our sisters. In addition, my own journey was profoundly affected by the assassination of Archbishop Oscar Romero and of the four U.S. churchwomen in El Salvador in 1980. My ministry in those years and for many years after was with immigrants, mostly people from Central America who were fleeing the violence there. I was very challenged by the recognition that our own government was fueling the war against these same people. Now the victims included a prophetic bishop and four women just like me. How could we respond to this violence? How would Jesus respond? The more I have accompanied the people themselves who are victims of violence and oppression — first Central Americans and, more recently, the people of the Middle East — the more I have been converted by their faith and example and found my own religious vocation shaped and challenged by their struggle for liberation.

Vocation to Mission

Another extraordinary encounter with vocation in my life has been through my work with Maryknoll women and men around the world — lay missioners, sisters, priests and brothers. Each is called to a particular expression of the vocation to cross-cultural mission, but all are called to mission — some for life; others for a specific period of time in their lives. The Maryknoll sisters are vowed members of a religious community in the Dominican tradition; the Maryknoll men make an oath for life as priests or brothers in the Catholic Foreign Mission Society of America; and Maryknoll lay missioners are married or single lay people whose commitment to Maryknoll is temporary, for about three years at a time. Maryknoll also welcomes shorter-term commitments to mission by diocesan priests, members of other religious communities, and lay affiliates.

I have seen Maryknoll missioners living and working in dozens of countries. I have heard their stories of vibrant and fulfilling life at the edge of life; bringing the Good News to far corners of the earth where they themselves were evangelized; encountering great beauty and goodness and terrible evil. I have seen them join with others to evangelize structures, including those of already-Christian institutions; evangelize cultures, including our own U.S. culture; evangelize systems, including political and economic systems locally and globally.

I have seen them play, and joined them in fiestas, where a "wonderful time was had by all" with very few amenities. I have seen their creativity, their theological depth, their passionate concern for the human community and for earth herself.

Meaningful Lives in Mission

In December of 2005 I took my then thirteen-year-old granddaughter to El Salvador for the twenty-fifth anniversary of the assassination of the four U.S. churchwomen in that country during the brutal Salvadoran civil war. The Maryknoll sisters still living in El Salvador had prepared a pilgrimage to celebrate the lives of the four women. It was the first time my granddaughter had spent any time with missioners or with women religious. Our days together were extremely intense. With many Salvadorans, we went to the tomb of Jesuit Rutilio Grande who, with his companions, a *campesino* and young boy, was murdered because he spoke out in favor of the dignity of poor people in his parish. We went to the chapel where Archbishop Oscar Romero was martyred a few months before the four women. We visited the garden at the University of Central America where six Jesuit priests, whose academic commitment was to the poor, were assassinated with two co-workers. We went to the cemetery where the two Maryknoll sisters are buried and to the rural site where the four women were so brutally murdered.

We both found the whole journey to be extremely moving. We were with dozens of Maryknoll sisters, most of whom knew very well the two Maryknoll martyrs, as well as Jean and Dorothy, and who retold their story in great detail. Those were holy days as we walked on sacred ground.

But four characteristics of the Maryknollers were especially striking, even to my young granddaughter: the depth and beauty of their love for El Salvador and the Salvadoran people; the importance that they gave to retelling the women's story as a story about life and fidelity to the gospel of life overcoming death; their insistence that the martyred women's commitment to solidarity be a model for us now and in the future, not an artifact of the past; and their ability to have a wonderful, joyful, hilarious time together.

Some years will pass before my granddaughter begins to make decisions about her vocation, but hopefully her experience during those few days in El Salvador added content and texture to the possibilities before her. She saw a quite lovely demonstration of the fact that giving your life to enhancing the well-being of people you love and to something you believe in deeply, as have all the sisters we were with in those days, can lead to a life of meaning, fulfillment, and joy.

In the reflection paper the Maryknoll sisters prepared for those who participated in the anniversary celebration, they described solidarity as a posture that is rooted in the identity of each person as a creature of God, a creature endowed with immense dignity, a treasure who is created for interdependence within our human and earth community. They called us to a spirituality of "family solidarity, which sets us free to transform our broken world." It is a spirituality that they themselves live.

Every Baptized Person Has a Calling

Father Mike Snyder, M.M., whose own mission experience was in Africa, mostly Tanzania, was in recent years vocation director for the Maryknoll Fathers and Brothers. When I asked him what he says to young men interested in joining Maryknoll, he wrote,

EVERY BAPTIZED PERSON has a calling in life! In the Catholic Church when speaking of calling we use the word "vocation."

Traditionally this meant a calling to the religious life. But this was quite myopic. God is alive within all the followers of Jesus Christ; if we are receptive, the Spirit of God will guide our steps and lead us on a path to happiness in this life.

Yes, each baptized person has a vocation, a calling in life. This should affect our professional choices as well as our personal ones. So as we look at educational pursuits or contemplate marriage, a family, etc., we are called to be attentive to God speaking to us through the experiences and people in our lives.

Over the years I have corresponded with thousands of young people who are searching for their vocation. Somehow they have heard about Maryknoll, who we are and what we do. They tell me that they have been nurtured in U.S. society to get a good education, a good job, material possessions, including a home, etc. They were told that would be the path to happiness. Many among them had achieved these goals, yet happiness had eluded them. They felt deceived and embarked on a journey in search of happiness.

They say that they were raised to think too much of themselves and not enough of others. Some get involved in volunteer work; others pursue service careers; many become grounded in a faith in Jesus. They have come to realize that God has something special in store for them: the chance to make a difference in the world with their lives.

In the course of our correspondence it becomes clear that a lifetime missionary career overseas is not for everyone, but those who wish to learn more seek nourishment for the journey as they listen to the Spirit of God at work within. And they are not afraid to take steps and gain experience. Several have asked to work with Maryknoll overseas during semester breaks or vacation in places like Cambodia, Thailand, Mozambique, Kenya, and Bolivia. Through these experiences the calling is refined — or they drop away. But others remain steadfast, recognizing that God is indeed calling them to the missionary life.

I feel that Maryknoll offers the greatest challenge to a Catholic priest: to give up one's culture, language, and way of life. But in this greatest challenge I believe that I will cultivate my faith in a loving God far beyond anything I could ever have imagined.

We are each called to listen to God's activity within our hearts. To truly hear can be a blessed experience, but it is not necessarily easy. It requires a posture of silence and peace. Many of us have become accustomed to noise and to constant activity. There is little silence in our lives; when there doesn't seem to be much to do, we search out activities, ways of filling in the gap and ending the silence. We need to embrace the silence to be attentive. This can be frightening as we realize that a leap of faith is required, that trusting in God may spiral us out into unknown areas of life. We are accustomed to having everything under control and planned well in advance. Often we need to learn about the "leap of faith" and what it entails. But when we do, when we do the proper work of discerning what is going on in our vocational journeys, when we take the leap, God's Spirit is revealed to us in amazing ways.

Lay Vocations to Mission

In my many years with Maryknoll I have participated in the orientation programs for new lay missioners, visited dozens and dozens of lay people in their mission sites in different corners of the world, and remained in contact with many after they left Maryknoll and followed their next vocational steps. They have been young and not so young, single and married, from a multitude of backgrounds and racial and ethnic groups. All were taking or had taken a leap of faith that thrust them into profoundly challenging and life-giving cross-cultural circumstances. All were forever changed by the experience.

Maryknoll lay missioner Susan Nagle, a medical doctor who has worked in Africa for over twenty years, wrote:

ALL OF MY EARLY LIFE I knew I had been blessed. I came from a good family, I had all my needs met, and I was able to choose my profession and practice what I enjoyed most: medicine. I had always been interested in people who didn't have the same opportunities, and my earliest remembrance was visiting my uncle, Fr. Joe Nagle, at the parish in Sunfish, Kentucky, where he worked as a Glenmary priest. The entire school was a one-room classroom and each row was a different grade! I went back to work in Appalachia several times and then on to Nicaragua and the Dominican Republic. By the time I finished my medical training I wanted to give back something of substance to people in a different culture who could use my services. I wanted to learn the language and culture and I knew that would take several years. I was, even then, thinking it might take a very long time. I wanted the support and camaraderie of my own faith tradition. I knew that would be important to my own growth and survival. And I wanted the opportunity to marry should the right man come along. The only group that offered all those possibilities in 1983/84 was the Maryknoll lay mission program.

Vocation, or calling, is a process. It never ends. Life is like a river, or a symphony, always on the move and ever-changing. I worked first in Tanzania. Then southern Sudan. Now Kenya. I've tried to keep listening to the small voice within, God calling. I've tried to do what God wants, although my own desires have, at times, been at odds with the path I was on. I have been disappointed, sick, and frustrated many times. But I have done things I never would have chosen or thought possible and have grown immensely. I have been very blessed by the people I have met, lived and worked with. And I am grateful for everything along the way. The essence of vocation is listening to God calling — and then responding. The reward is life.

Vocation to Marriage

On the threshold of his public life Jesus performs his first sign, at his mother's request, during a wedding feast. The church attaches great importance to Jesus' presence at the wedding at Cana. She sees in it the confirmation of the goodness of marriage and the proclamation that thenceforth marriage will be an efficacious sign of Christ's presence.[24]

Marriage, I believe, is a sacred vocation to which some are called. It is an invitation into a particular version of community that is both demanding and life-giving, nurturing and challenging. Marriages, I think, like snowflakes or fingerprints, are uniquely molded by the individual human beings who become life partners, enabling them to fully realize their own potential and to help birth a better world by who they are together.

Perhaps one of the most satisfying experiences of my own life has been to see my children build life-giving, mutually respectful, and enduring relationships. They grew into adulthood absorbing lessons from a society in transition, often painful transition, toward greater equality between women and men. They experienced many different models of relationship at home and as their horizons were deliberately expanded in diverse communities and challenging educational settings. We worked very hard among ourselves to shape deep, loving, challenging, and respectful familial relationships. I had learned hard lessons about the need for good communication skills and we tried to hone them together, the children and I, after I found myself a single parent.

Their descriptions of marriage are testimony to the gift and challenge of that noble vocation. One couple wrote:

MARRIAGE IS THE BEGINNING of unconditional love, love without a tally sheet, an attempt to make the other person be all he or she can be. We feel there is a bond in marriage that frees us to be as true to ourselves and therefore to one another as possible, always. Always, because the commitment we made in marriage was about true honesty and fulfillment. This is the essence of married life for us, and it provides us with one of many gifts of married life. Marriage itself is a gift, the gift that waits at the end of every real struggle, either out "in the world" or within the marriage itself. The promise we made to each other also gives us the gifts of peace, security, and happiness, and the challenge to seek our true calling in life.

And the most beautiful gifts of all from our marriage are our four children. The challenges of marriage are also numerous. The beauty of finding your perfect complement can also be very ugly at times! Growing, trying day after day to be better than you were yesterday, is why we are all here, but it can be hard. To discuss, compromise, coordinate, and collaborate with another human being every day, to make time for our relationship, to purposefully carve out time in schedule after schedule for only each other can also be challenging, especially for those of us inclined to charge through life at full throttle! But staying connected requires that we meet the challenges.

Another said:

THE WORD THAT I THINK OF most often when I think of marriage as a life or a vocation is "home." In many ways, I see marriage as the making of a home, the conscious choice to create a home with someone else. It's a commitment to share a space and a life grounded in a shared commitment. In marriage, we find not just the private, intimate love or the public, shared commitment, but a grounded confidence in a shared life, a shared home.

Another:

TO BE A PARTNER in marriage is to stand ready to accompany and to be accompanied. It is not about merging or blending, but about walking firmly forward in each other's company. It is about each celebrating the other's strengths and unique gifts without needing to compete. We see something magic emerge as our marriage ages. The magic has to do with the inverse of loneliness, the confidence of having a friend, a friend we like to be with, to talk with, to think with, and the pleasure of being confident that the conversation will start from the same basic values. Challenges don't come to mind readily, only those challenges of relationship, the push and shove of communication, remembering to listen and to be kind, remembering to take time in the midst of everything else to be together, the challenge of compromise.

Another:

THE COMMITMENT BETWEEN two people to offer love and support for the duration of their lives is something that we cherish more than anything else. We believe that marriage is a challenge to excel in every way possible in making sure that your partner is encouraged to take risks, supported when risks don't pan out, celebrated when things are going well, and above all loved with all your heart. Although many say it is unconditional love, the truth really is that marriage is a commitment to have conditions or expectations and challenges on love, conditions that are possible to achieve and instantly adapted when needs arise. An example of a condition is to challenge each other to live our lives with a sense of purpose, constantly remembering we are in the world to be of service to others and to build relationships with people making the world a more positive place. Another example is to expect that we treat each other with respect. The love between two people in a marriage must be strong enough to endure mere differences in opinions as well as compassionate enough to wait for hours for an opinion even to develop. The foundation of our marriage is a balance of friendship, love, respect, and trust, a balance that is not stagnant. We continuously make adjustments and corrections to maintain this balance. We believe that justice within marriage, within our personal day-to-day relationship, is a step toward building peace and justice in this world. We believe that without love and justice in the home, we cannot achieve broader social and global justice. We want our marriage to reflect the peace and justice we seek for the world. Marriage for us is not only personal. It is also political. Being married, we are public about our most personal and intimate relationship. And it is about society acknowledging and accepting our choice to be together, to love each other, and to be intimate with each other. We are conscious that this is not a reality for all members of our community, which reminds us of the need to continue working for justice for all people. We see our childless marriage as a responsible choice and our contribution toward a more just and peaceful society, where diverse and varied forms of families are welcomed, respected, and protected.

And one more:

MARRIAGE MEANS WE GET TO SPEND every day with our best friend. We appreciate who we are as individuals and don't take each other for granted. We think communication is very important and we work on that daily. We support and respect each other. And most importantly we love each other, have fun together, and laugh every day.

Vocation to Parenting: Roots and Wings

The vocation to parenting has, I believe, as many faces as marriage and every other vocation. It is one way, but not the only way, we welcome, protect, and nurture new life.

Some of us are called to biological parenthood; others receive children into their lives by adoption or step-parenting or foster-parenting, by opening their hearts and homes to children in need, by being loving uncles and aunts.

Some are called to life-giving, nurturing relationships many times over in one generation; yet others, in succeeding generations. One of my heroines is Miss Virginia, a grandmother who used to live next door to Assisi Community in Washington, DC. Virginia was raising the five children of one of her daughters who at that time was struggling with an addiction to drugs. The unwavering stability and love that she offered those children was a shining light in our rough neighborhood.

How many like her in our city and around the world are parenting their children's children, thanks too often to war or street violence or deadly disease? There are 15 million children in the world who have lost one or both parents to AIDS.[25] They are being raised by grandparents, by older relatives, by siblings who themselves are still children, by strangers.

The mountain of "how to" advice for parents, as important and helpful as it may be, somehow skirts the essence of parenting as a *vocation, a calling.* Yet my many years of experience — with six children, four foster children (one of whom was part of our family for many years), and now grandchildren — has taught me that is exactly what parenting is: a *vocation.* And it is fertile soil for reflection on right relationships, community, the calling forth of charisma, humility, service, and the gifts of the Holy Spirit (especially wisdom, understanding, and fortitude), that I believe make faithful parenting possible.

At the heart of the Judeo-Christian tradition lies a vision of right relationships. In fact, the concepts of Sabbath, sabbatical year, and jubilee, which were given significant attention in 2000 at the turn of the millennium, and Jesus' own persistent message about right relationships within an inclusive discipleship community provide a solid foundation for this vocation.

Parents, I believe, are called to provide a rich experience of right relationships for their children. By owning and living out a belief in the essential dignity and value of each person, every child of God, and a deep respect for the integrity of creation, parents help young people develop a sense of their own essential value, an understanding of what "right relationship" means and the holy habit of living in right relationship with all other people and the rest of creation.

Second, I believe that a parent's vocation is to create community and to share with and demonstrate for their children essential lessons about community and the common good. In societies where individualism is emphasized, where *my* desires, *my* success, *my* victories, *my* fulfillment are considered most important, faith-filled parenting has to offer an alternative. Helping children to experience and contribute to the richness of the common life in a family community and to gradually expand that experience to other communities, including to the global community, is an essential responsibility of a parent's vocation.

In the introduction I wrote a few words about a booklet, *The Calling Forth of Charisma*, written several years ago by Elizabeth O'Connor, which said so much to me about another dimension of the vocation of parenting. "Charisma" refers to the essential character or special qualities of a particular person. To help young people recognize and nurture their own charisma is, in many ways, encouraging them to listen to the movement of the Spirit in their own lives and to risk following their own vocations.

Other characteristics of the parenting vocation, including humility and service, seem obvious, but Jesus' visit to the home of his disciples early in the Gospel of Mark sheds new light on those particular virtues:

> As soon as they left the synagogue, they entered the house of Simon and Andrew, with James and John. Now Simon's mother-in-law was in bed with a fever, and they told him about her at once. He came and took her by the hand and lifted her up. Then the fever left her and she began to serve them. (Mark 1:29–31)

In *Say to This Mountain* with biblical scholar Ched Myers we wrote,

> Peter's mother-in-law is the first woman to appear in Mark's narrative. We are told that upon being touched by Jesus, "she served him" (1:31). Most commentators, steeped in patriarchal theology, assume that this means she fixed Jesus dinner. However the Greek verb "to serve" (from which we get our word "deacon") appears only two other times in Mark. One is in 10:45 — "The Human One came not to be served but to serve" — a context hardly suggesting meal preparation....

The other comes at the end of the story, where Mark describes women "who, when Jesus was in Galilee, followed him, and served him, and . . . came up to Jerusalem with him" (15:41). This is a summary statement of discipleship: from beginning (Galilee) to end (Jerusalem) these women were true followers who, unlike the men (see 10:32–45), practiced servant-hood.[26]

Humility and service, when rightly understood, are not self-effacing characteristics, but virtues that depict a deep understanding of Jesus' message, true discipleship.

When practiced by parents, these virtues can convey to youngsters the importance of honesty about our own gifts and limitations and an understanding that no one person has the corner on all the truth. I once read that parents have to go 90 percent of the distance to meet their children half-way — and we have to go that distance without the kind of arrogance that undercuts good relationships.

So many other Gospel stories speak to me clearly about the long and challenging journey of those who are called to parenting and the gifts of the Spirit that make parenting possible: wisdom, understanding, and fortitude.

"Then Joseph got up, took the child and his mother by night and went to Egypt and remained there until the death of Herod" (Matt. 2:14). Millions of parents in our own times flee with their loved ones from war and violent conflict, from repression, from hunger and poverty. Millions of others migrate on their own, sending home remittances that alone make survival for their children possible.

"And the child's father and mother were amazed at what was being said about him. Then Simeon blessed them and said to his mother Mary, 'This child is destined for the falling and the rising of many in Israel, and to be a sign that will be opposed so that the inner thoughts of many will be revealed — and a sword will pierce your own soul too'" (Luke 2:33–35). And "meanwhile, standing near the cross of Jesus were his mother and his mother's sister, Mary the wife of Clopas, and Mary Magdalene" (John 19:25). I have not lived this ultimate agony of a parent, but so many have: the parents of the martyrs for justice and peace known to our generation — the parents of Ita Ford, Jean Donovan, Maura Clarke, Dorothy Kazel, Rachel Corrie, Celina Ramos, Ben Linder; the parents of the victims on all sides of all wars; the parents of the victims of genocide; the parents of the children who die of hunger or treatable disease....

Now every year his parents went to Jerusalem for the festival of the Passover. And when he was twelve years old, they went up as usual for the festival. When the festival was ended and they started to return, the boy Jesus stayed behind in Jerusalem, but his parents did not know it. Assuming that he was in the group of travelers, they went a day's journey. Then they started to look for him among their relatives and friends. When they did not find him, they returned to Jerusalem to search for him. After three days they found him in the temple, sitting among the teachers, listening to them and asking them questions. All who heard him were amazed at his understanding and his answers. When his parents saw him, they were astonished, and his mother said to him, "Child, why have you treated us like this? Look, your father and I have been searching for you in great anxiety." He said to them, "Why were you searching for me? Did you not know that I must be in my Father's house?" But they did not understand what he said to them. Then he went down with them and came to Nazareth, and was obedient to them. His mother treasured all these things in her heart. (Luke 2:41–52)

Giving our children roots makes sense to many of us parents, but I believe it is much more difficult to give them wings — to trust, love, and affirm them into responsible adulthood, to accept the important decisions they make, and to celebrate their move to become subjects of their own lives.

Parenting Our Parents

In many cultures, probably since the beginning of the human story, families and extended families have been centers of mutual physical, psychological, and spiritual support from birth until the end of life as we know it. Some families and some cultures have shaped that support more substantially, more thickly, than others.

Many families have faced together almost insurmountable obstacles to secure a dignified life. Others have dealt with deep dysfunction and violence at the heart of the family unit. The experience of families and extended families is neither new nor homogenous, and often it is not easy.

But in some, especially wealthier, cultures, including our own, the intersection of longer life expectancies (people living well into their nineties) and the geographical separation of extended families is presenting new challenges and new opportunities for many of us.

Giving our children roots makes sense to many of us parents, but I believe it is much more difficult to give them wings.

For almost seven years, from the time my mother was eighty-eight until she died a few weeks short of her ninety-fifth birthday, I had the graced opportunity to live with her and to accompany her on the long journey home to God. We had lived together periodically over the years since I "left home." My oldest daughter, who was her first grandchild, and I had moved home for several months after my dad died very suddenly at age fifty-seven; later, when "Grand" retired she lived with us on the farm and provided an oasis of calm and dignity in the chaos of our hurly-burly brood of children and animals; and when I found myself juggling frantically to regain my balance as a recently single mom, she was a regular lifesaver for me personally and for our whole family.

But, as so many adult children know well, the last years of her life were unique, special, and particularly challenging. The vocation of caretaker was both deeply rewarding and extremely difficult. It taught me lessons I didn't know I had to learn, redefined my understanding of marginalization, stripped me in ways that raising six children never did, and at times demanded more than I was able to give in terms of time, attention, communication, and understanding.

I gained enormous respect for those who give their lives to healing and caretaking ministries. As my mom's strength and engagement in life began to wane, I found myself ill equipped to respond in a helpful way. I had been totally comfortable and self-assured raising children with vastly different needs and personalities. I had no problem pushing them beyond where they thought they could go to experience a broken world and find ways to be a positive presence in it, helping to shape a better future. I expected and was blessed with self-confident children who became open-minded, critically thinking adults who are engaged in life in a wide variety of positive ways.

My mom had been the same: active, caring about others, always learning, even adventurous. But in her last years she began moving into another space that was foreign to her and to me. Neither of us knew how to navigate the physical challenges and even less the psychological and spiritual ones. As her world narrowed I often found myself caught on a small planet with her, desperately trying to push back the boundaries, to breathe back into her the joie de vivre I had known for so many years.

In retrospect I tried to keep her alive for as long as she was alive. I tried to help when help was really needed. I vowed not to do for her what she could very well do for herself and never to relate to her in any other way than as a mature adult who was fully subject of her own life.

When she and I moved in together, I moved out of Assisi Community and began to lose the sharp, principled edges of the "simple lifestyle" I had been trying to create for so many years. We made a home that was Grand's space, in which she would feel comfortable. I cooked different food, often buying expensive meat to see if I could tempt her aging palate, rather than the vegetarian fare to which I had been committed. The vocation to socially conscious living that I had believed was to be part of my journey forever felt like it was slipping out of reach, confronting me with an even deeper challenge.

I also began to feel that all the parenting skills I had developed were no longer useful. Even that vocation, which had been so central to my life for forty years, felt strangely outdated. Instead of accompanying my children from dependence to maturity and independence, I was called to accompany my mother from maturity and independence to dependence. Instead of challenging my children to move their centers of gravity outside of themselves to dance the dance of life with a broken world, I was called to walk with my mom as her center of gravity moved away from a broken world back into herself and finally to another world. It was a vocation that required letting go in a manner that was more demanding than letting go of suburban living, letting go of the farm, letting go of my children as they grew up, letting go of my own house, even letting go of beauty when I moved into the dilapidated houses of Assisi Community. It felt like this vocation was asking me to let go of my values and my dreams of moving to the margins to accompany the poor.

But on this bumpy road as I was trying to find my way, my spiritual director helped bring a bit of light on the horizon.

I had always thought of marginalization in terms of poverty. I was acutely aware of my own privileged access to a life of comfort and power in comparison to the majority of people in the world and of the gap between the rich and the poor. The question that had defined my own spiritual and vocational journey was, "What is the role of white, middle-class people of faith when the poor reach out to take what is rightfully theirs?" One answer was to try to move my own life and my family in the context of community to the side of the poor — physically, politically, vocationally.

This journey of many years and different vocations has convinced me that our God is full of surprises, that she invites us to follow in ways that we don't expect or understand into places we had not planned to go.

But this new vocation of parent-care was asking of me something that seemed completely different and quite the opposite — until I began to reflect on the position of the elderly in a society fixated on staying young and, at all costs, trying to avoid death. Though accompanying my mom in her last years seemed to be a move away from the margins, I came to see it as a different set of steps in the same direction I had been heading for so many years — toward the margins.

But those steps were, in fact, even harder than ones I had tried to take before. To slow down my own pace of life, which for decades had been pretty frantic just keeping up with a growing family, life in an intentional community, and demanding work for social justice and peace, was a challenging exercise in letting go. I can remember having to learn to *slow down* just walking from one end of the room to another with Grand or to *sit down and visit, to listen* when I got home, rather than rushing into preparations for dinner or other chores.

The other essential dimension of this vocation was that it had to be lived in community, in this instance, family community. I have one sister whose deep involvement in our mother's care made it possible for me to continue to work full time and to travel as needed for work during the years Grand and I lived together. The weeks that she took over the work of mother-care also helped me regain my bearings and sort out next steps on the journey.

My children, their spouses, and my grandchildren also were deeply involved in this family vocation. They were constantly trying to figure out how to make it possible for their grandmother/great-grandmother to stay at the center of our family's activities. Often their activities were moved to where she was. As her health and strength deteriorated, they found ways to include her and to make her comfortable and at home with them. When I could not leave her alone and could not be home myself, they came and cooked and kept her company and helped with her personal care. When the need was for woman-help, daughters and daughters-in-law came to the rescue. When the need was for other kinds of help, everyone showed up as much as they possibly could.

Assisi Community also took on a piece of this vocation. They provided spiritual and moral support for both of us, morning after morning at 6:30 a.m. I would show up at Assisi for half an hour of prayer and soul-space. They were friends for her, including her for as long as she was able in community activities. The last time she was at Assisi Community was just a few weeks before she died, when she was carried into the house for Assisi's twentieth anniversary celebration. And they were a support for me, filling in gaps in the Grand-care schedule whenever I began to panic.

Parenting our parents is a very old vocation, but, at least in U.S. culture, one set in a new and changing context. This sacred call eliminates any illusions that vocation refers to a once-in-a-lifetime event or is limited to early-in-life experiences.

Our God Is Full of Surprises

This journey of many years and different vocations has convinced me that our God is full of surprises, that she invites us to follow in ways that we don't expect or understand into places we had not planned to go. I am convinced as well that the vocation to discipleship is often repeated; we have many opportunities to catch the cadence of God's voice.

Occasionally, we feel like we're jumping off a cliff when we say yes, taking a risk that seems overwhelming. We thought we were settled for life, with no more major decisions to make, and then we realized that we were facing a challenge or an opportunity that would stretch us one more time farther than we thought we could go to follow Jesus.

But most of the time we simply take the next right step, not huge steps either, just one at a time. And when we look back a few years down the road, a pattern of "call and response" begins to become visible. Rarely, especially as adults, were we sitting around waiting for an invitation, but God called nonetheless — through loved ones and community, through neighbors, through a broken and hungry world, through the beauty or the cry of creation.

> As he was walking along he saw Levi, son of Alphaeus, sitting at the tax booth, and he said to him, "Follow me." And he got up and followed him. (Mark 2:14)

_____

Chapter Three

Called to Happiness

The Beatitudes reveal the goal of human existence, the ultimate end of human acts: God calls us to his own beatitude. This vocation is addressed to each individual personally, but also to the church as a whole, the new people made up of those who have accepted the promise and live from it in faith.[27]

MATTHEW (chapters 5–7) and Luke (chapter 6), in their accounts of the Jesus story, both include the details of the Christian vocation laid out by Jesus in the long Sermon on the Mount. Matthew wrote:

Blessed are the poor in spirit, for theirs is the kingdom of heaven.

Blessed are they who mourn, for they will be comforted.

Blessed are the meek, for they will inherit the earth.

Blessed are they who hunger and thirst for righteousness [justice], for they will be filled.

Blessed are the merciful, for they will receive mercy.

Blessed are the pure in heart, for they will see God.

Blessed are the peacemakers, for they will be called children of God.

*Blessed are they who are persecuted for righteousness'
[justice'] sake, for theirs is the kingdom of heaven.*

*Blessed are you when people revile you and persecute you
and utter all kinds of evil against you falsely on my
account.*

*Rejoice and be glad for your reward is great in heaven, for
in the same way they persecuted the prophets who were
before you.* (Matt. 5:1–10)

Luke's account is similar, but with a different emphasis:

*Blessed are you who are poor, for yours is the kingdom of
God.*

*Blessed are you who are now hungry, for you will be
filled.*

Blessed are you who weep now, for you will laugh.

*Blessed are you when people hate you, and when they
exclude, revile you and defame you on account of the Son
of Man.*

*Rejoice in that day and leap for joy, for surely your reward
is great in heaven; for that is what their ancestors did to
the prophets.*

*But woe to you who are rich, for you have received your
consolation.*

Woe to you who are full now, for you will be hungry.

*Woe to you who are laughing now, for you will mourn and
weep.*

*Woe to you when all speak well of you, for that is what their
ancestors did to the false prophets.* (Luke 6:20–26)

God calls us to a fundamental orientation, an option for discipleship, that sets the stage on which we dance the dance of life and promises happiness (Blessed are you...) to those who heed the call.

> The beatitude we are promised confronts us with decisive moral choices.... It teaches us that true happiness is not found in riches or well-being, in human fame or power, or in any human achievement — however beneficial it may be — such as science, technology, and art, or indeed in any creature, but in God alone, the source of every good and of all love.[28]

Beatitude, the fulfillment of the Promise, the "already and the not yet," is the heart of the gospel message. Jesus proclaimed the in-breaking of the Reign of God: "Today, this Scripture has been fulfilled in your hearing" (Luke 4:21), and he lived as if that were true, demonstrating for his disciples and all who could "see," the pathway to inclusive community, right relationships, and the New Creation, the Reign of God.

Though the stage on which we move through the journey of life may seem stable, though we may have already proclaimed *I have decided to follow Jesus,* the stage settings often change, sometimes dramatically, in response to the multiple opportunities and invitations of a lifetime.

Jesus' Sermon on the Mount lays out a moral framework for vocational decisions in response to these invitations. By his powerful preaching and by his own life, he emphasized over and over again the privileged place of impoverished and excluded peoples; the great need for compassion and social comforting; the centrality to the discipleship journey of the work for social justice or righteousness; and the call to peace-making and reconciliation. In this chapter we will explore the diversity of vocations this framework suggests.

Celebration of life in God (*Blessed are you.... Happy are you . . .*), celebration that *is* life in God, the paradoxical prom-ises, the blessings and rewards, the already and the not yet will be the centerpiece of the last chapter.[29]

The Privileged Place of Those Who Are Poor

We move to the side of those who are poor so as to hear the cadence of God's call, and the discipleship vocation we dis-cern there may well keep us poor, or at least living in solidarity with those who are poor for the long haul.

Let me paint for you a few pictures of this poverty that is in some way connected to blessedness. As I do so, paint your own vignettes as well.

The first is of a desert in Arizona: water bottles are strewn across the landscape in every direction; in the background is a small cemetery in which a number of crosses are marked "unknown." Fearful people are moving along unclear trails. Their families were left behind in Ecuador, Peru, Bolivia, Guatemala, Nicaragua, El Salvador, Mexico, in China, the Sudan, Rwanda, the Democratic Republic of the Congo, Chad. They have heard horrific stories about people suffo-cating in closed railroad cars and trucks, dying of heat stroke in the desert, getting lost, going in circles. Yet they come from all over the world to attempt this dangerous crossing. Most of them left communities where their future was looking more and more dismal, hoping to find a job and thereby to support their loved ones. They are from impoverished communities in impoverished countries. They are among the most marginalized people wherever they go. They are the very poor. Blessed are they.

We move to the side of those who are poor so as to hear the cadence of God's call, and the discipleship vocation we discern there may well keep us poor, or at least living in solidarity with those who are poor for the long haul.

The second image is from the other side of the world, from Phnom Penh, Cambodia. Many families there live on palettes, large tables that mark off one family's space from that of their neighbor. Imagine there a mother and three children. The father has already died of AIDS. The mother is now dying; her seven-year-old son is caring for her, and for his two younger siblings. The little boy is HIV positive. Unlike his parents, he may have access to antiretroviral medicines, but that access is far from guaranteed, and he will need them for life. This seven-year-old and his brother and sister also are the very poor. They will struggle, probably for the rest of their lives, to find water, food, a place to live. They may never go to school, and if they do, even a good education may not help them find a decent job. Blessed are they.

A third image is from the eastern part of the Democratic Republic of the Congo, where thirty or forty young men have found refuge for a few months in a center for former child soldiers. They are among the hundreds of thousands of children under the age of eighteen who have been forcibly recruited or lured by promises of enough to eat to serve in government forces or armed rebel groups. Some are as young as eight years old. They are both boys and girls. Children like them have been caught in armed conflicts in almost every region of the world. They serve as porters or cooks, guards, messengers or spies. Sometimes they are forced to the front lines, sent into minefields ahead of older troops or used for suicide missions. Many were forced to commit atrocities against their own family or neighbors; they are "stigmatized" and many are unable to return home. They are the very poor. Blessed are they.

And a last image is from the United States, from a neighborhood in our nation's capital, only a few blocks from the White House, where a grandmother and her five grandchildren live crammed in a small, dangerous basement apartment because they cannot afford anything better; where on any given night homeless shelters are full of men, women, and children who can't afford even one room; where the hundreds of people who don't fit or are unwilling to go into the shelters sleep on heating vents on public sidewalks or in cars, even in the middle of winter. Many of them work long hours but still don't earn enough to secure decent housing or health care. They are another face of the very poor. Blessed are they.

Poverty, according to the thesaurus, is scarcity, shortage, deficiency, lack, destitution, indigence, need. Poverty is privation at the most basic level of human need: lack of food, clothing, shelter, health care, education; it precludes the possibility of a life that is fully human.

Blessed are the poor, for they shall be called children of God...

One of the clearest measures of beatitude is poverty, poverty that is both real and relational. Blessed are the poor themselves and blessed are the poor in spirit.

Pope Paul VI in *Populorum Progressio* wrote about basic poverty at the root of what he called "less human conditions":[30] the lack of material necessities for those who are without the minimum essentials for life. Migrants, the children in Cambodia, child soldiers, those who are impoverished in a world of wealth.

Blessed are they who lack the basic necessities for a decent life.

In the same paragraph the Holy Father wrote about "the moral deficiencies of those who are mutilated by selfishness." He called their reality "less human conditions" as well, and called those living in conditions of this moral deficiency to turn "toward the spirit of poverty," to live in solidarity with those who are now poor.

Blessed are the poor in spirit, for theirs is the kingdom of heaven.

The vocation to be poor in spirit is, I believe, much, much more challenging than we are often led to believe. Being poor in spirit moves us beyond "detachment" from the material possessions we continue to accumulate toward real simplicity of lifestyle and into relationship with those who are impoverished and living on the margins of our societies.

To be poor in spirit we have to believe in the equal dignity of every person in the eyes of God and act accordingly. If what we have, where we live, how we spend, or don't spend, our time keeps us from having friends who are poor, then we need to rethink what we have, where we live, and how we spend our time.

To be poor in spirit we have to "live simply so that others may simply live" (Gandhi). If what we have or eat or wear is produced by workers who are not paid a living wage, then we have to change what we have or eat or wear.

To be poor in spirit we have to live the virtue of solidarity, accompany the poor — next door and on the other side of the world — and interpret reality from their perspective. If we begin to think everyone can get out of poverty by trying harder, we have to rethink our analysis of the world in which we live.

To be poor in spirit we have to work with those who are poor to change the structures and transform the systems that create or perpetuate poverty. We have to evaluate laws and public policy proposals and business practices by what they do *to* people who are poor, what they do *for* people who are poor, and what they *enable* poor people to do for themselves.

To be poor in spirit we have to make detachment from material possessions an essential characteristic of our individual, family and community lifestyles. We cannot define who we are by what we have or how much we earn.

To be poor in spirit we have to be careful about how we earn money, how we do or do not accumulate wealth, how we use resources. The way we earn a living has to measure up to the standards of the gospel and Catholic social teaching. So does every decision to invest and in what. By this vocation we are accountable to the poorest people in our global community for how we use time and talent and financial resources.

If what we have or eat or wear is produced by workers who are not paid a living wage, then we have to change what we have or eat or wear.

To be poor in spirit we have to live in a manner that is *conscious* of the reality in which most people live; we have to understand the systemic and structural connections between our prosperity and others' poverty.

To be poor in spirit we have to shape our lives and our futures from the standpoint and for the sake of those who are poor.

But how does this vocation — to be poor in spirit, this privileged place of poor people — intersect with other *calls* we have heard, the call to parenting, for example, or the call to a single life or the call to teaching, to mission, to medicine? Is this call of Jesus, this foundational theme in the Beatitudes, reserved for a chosen few?

That only a few should care about the poor clearly was not the message of the Sermon on the Mount, but to live in solidarity with those who are poor, to be poor in spirit with all that vocation implies remains a tremendous challenge for followers of Jesus who, like the rich young man in the Gospel have "many possessions" or already busy lives (Mark 10:23).

At the same time, evidence abounds that many people of faith, Catholics among them, take this call very seriously. Many examples come to mind. Some are formal programs but many are woven into everyday lessons in families across the country.

Every parent, I suspect, tries to instill in their child an awareness that all the children in the world don't have hundreds of choices in breakfast cereal or the latest computer or even a house to live in. I believe deeply that teaching children to live simply, modeling for them how to live with less on a daily basis in a consumer society, is one of the greatest gifts we can give them.

Choosing to live in neighborhoods and towns that are economically diverse, where people with vastly different means live side by side, where their children go to school together and play together, where employers and employees know each other as human beings, and where people commit themselves to the common good is another.

To work toward a society where such an integrated way of life is even possible may be a vocation in itself.

Other, more structured approaches to living in solidarity with those who are poor, to being poor in spirit, include, for example, service-learning, alternative spring break and immersion programs for Catholic high school and college students. Teachers, counselors, parents, social workers, pastoral workers, bus drivers, administrators and their staff members, and students themselves spend significant human and other resources ensuring that young people encounter poverty with its disastrous impact on the lives it touches and that they have some idea of how to respond.

Many programs do an excellent job of helping the students reflect on their experience and incorporate it into their vocational decision-making process. Beyond serving poor people and their communities in some way, students are encouraged to ask why the poverty they touched and were touched by exists, what are its root causes and how to respond effectively. The hope is that such an experience will have a lasting impact on the students, ultimately leading them to spend their lives conscious of and responding to the scandal of poverty.

Parish twinning and solidarity programs also create opportunities for people to explore what being poor in spirit might mean in their lives through a brief overseas or "other side of the city" experience and ongoing mutually beneficial relationships with communities living in vastly different social realities.

Some, both religious and lay people, volunteers and missioners, who live for longer periods of time outside of the United States or in very poor U.S. communities are radically changed by an encounter with deep poverty and with the poor in huge numbers. Many of them have a particular vocation to "reverse mission," bringing home a worldview from the perspective of those who are poor in our country or our world.

Whatever vocation they are living, they are dramatically affected by that encounter and frequently ask themselves how what they are doing with their lives is affecting or could affect the poorest of the poor. That is the vocational question we each have to ask.

Moving as Communities to the Side of Those Who Are Poor

The vocation of humanity is to show forth the image of God and to be transformed into the image of the [God's] only Son. This vocation takes a personal form since each of us is called to enter into the divine beatitude; it also concerns the human community as a whole.[31]

In the years after the Second Vatican Council, the Catholic Church in Latin America deliberately shifted its social location from the side of the rich and powerful to make what came to be known as a preferential option for the poor. Articulated officially for the first time in 1968 at the meeting in Medellín, Colombia, of the Latin American Catholic Bishops Conference (CELAM), this movement of the church *as an institution,* profoundly affected the worldview and ministry of clergy and lay people across the continent.

This transformation of the church to accompany poor and excluded people physically (pastoral workers literally moved into *barrios* and *favelas* to experience the reality that the poor lived) was deeply rooted in faith. It was an effort to answer the question: What does the gospel have to say to people living in inhuman conditions? It was an effort to *be* Good News for impoverished and often oppressed people, to assure them of their inherent worth and dignity, to encourage them to be subjects of their own lives, to participate in efforts to change the miserable reality in which they were living, to expect more social justice in this life, not only waiting until the next for their eternal reward.

It was a direct and powerful application of the central principle of Catholic social teaching — the dignity of the human person — and of another principle of Catholic social teaching: that we are persons in community. How we locate our lives, our communities, our work, our institutions has to do with our communal vocation to move to the side of those who are poor as followers of Jesus.

Our community in Washington, DC, Assisi Community, is not poor. We have a place to call home, food, jobs, a measure of security. When we founded the community in 1986 we moved into two big old row houses in a poor and quite marginal part of Washington. We lived there as neighbors, struggling with unwanted four-legged creatures in the alley, petty drug trafficking, more than a measure of violence and mediocre city services. Then the housing boom hit the city and a metro station opened at the end of our block. The neighborhood began to gentrify. If our poor neighbors who were renting rooms and apartments were forced out of the neighborhood because the owners of the houses in which they lived could make a huge profit by selling the houses out from under them, what should Assisi Community do? There was no easy answer, but it became clear that we had to take the question seriously.

Blessed are the poor. . . . Blessed are the poor in spirit. . . .

What does that mean for us as a community? Any move would be expensive and perhaps our staying in the neighborhood would slow the gentrification and make it possible for others of modest means to stay. On the other hand, the daily challenges of living in a poor neighborhood had been very important to our community's growth and vision. The only clarity was in the complexity of the question.

We live in a time of what must be unprecedented disparity between the earning potential of one person in comparison to another. Put aside for a moment the billion people in the world who live on less than a dollar a day (the family in Cambodia, the families of the child soldiers in the Democratic Republic of the Congo, people migrating in search of decent work) or who never receive a regular paycheck. Consider only the reality of the working poor, those in the United States who work full time at the federal minimum wage and earn about $15,000 per year. What would it mean for those of us whose earning potential is much higher than that to be poor in spirit in relation to someone earning the minimum wage? In relation to someone who works long days but cannot afford a decent place to live (the grandmother in Washington)?

Blessed are the poor. . . . Blessed are the poor in spirit. . . .

What does that mean for us as individuals and families? Clearly, there is a diversity of vocations within this vocation, but take it seriously we must.

Compassion for Those Who Mourn

Blessed are they who mourn, for they will be comforted. Blessed are you who are now weeping, for you will laugh.

Just in my own lifetime, the world has lived through war, genocide, and brutal repression that collectively have taken millions of lives. Every one was beloved. So was each person victimized by the Nazi holocaust (6 million dead), the killing fields of Cambodia (2 million dead), the Rwandan genocide (800,000 dead), the war in Bosnia-Herzogovina (200,000 dead), the rape of Nanking (300,000 dead), Stalin's forced famine (7 million dead), the slaughter of Armenians in Turkey (1.5 million dead), the massacres in 626 Mayan communities during the civil war in Guatemala, the massacres of El Mozote and the Sumpul River in El Salvador, the slaughter in Darfur — and, tragically, on and on.

A voice was heard in Ramah, wailing and loud lamentation, Rachel weeping for her children; she refused to be consoled, because they are no more. (Matt. 2:18)

Blessed are they who mourn, for they will be comforted.
(Matt. 5:4)

In June of 2002 I had the privilege of visiting Afghanistan, where I met an eight-year-old girl named Amena. Amena was in the kitchen when bombs aimed at the Taliban or Al Qaeda struck her house near Kanduz, Afghanistan. Her mother, her brothers, her sisters, her cousins, her aunt and her uncle were killed, sixteen people in all, including a two-day-old baby. Her father survived but with horrendous physical and emotional injuries. The bombs went terribly awry — the closest Taliban were six miles away — but regrets about a serious targeting error will not bring back Amena's family. She and the survivors of war around the world know what it means to mourn.

Often we who are far from such atrocities are little aware of the mourning that they evoke. We may think about the horror and the presence of evil. We may not close our eyes to the brutality, but to ask what vocation means in this context is another challenging question.

Just a few weeks before the war in Afghanistan began, planes had careened into the soul of U.S. Americans in a manner previously unthinkable, immediately bringing life and death, truth and our vulnerability into sharp focus, and a powerful experience of mourning to our whole nation. The events of September 11, 2001, were catastrophic in a very real and a powerfully symbolic sense. Understanding a vocation to a world in mourning becomes a little more possible when a horror like 9/11 strikes closer to home.

Blessed are those who mourn; happy are those who mourn; they shall be comforted.

We have mourned at the sudden, or not so sudden, death, injury, or serious illness of a loved one or a neighbor, the loss of a job or an important relationship. We have tried to comfort others who are mourning. We have responded with compassion.

A vocation to compassion — to feel strong emotion with another person, empathy, sympathy, concern — is a social vocation as well as a personal one. Compassion requires that we not only "feel with" the other, but that, wherever possible, we participate in the transformation of situations causing the mourning.

A vocation shaped by this beatitude would work for an end to street violence, war and genocide, to hunger and famine, to premature death from preventable or treatable diseases. Compassion would become passion for peace-building, non-violent conflict resolution, food security, ecological integrity, affordable health care. Compassion would become a passion for right relationships, for social and ecological justice.

For a short while after 9/11, there was an intense rethinking of our priorities as a people, of what we really value. The scenes in the rubble of the World Trade Center and the Pentagon revealed what was important in life: not economic or military power or rank or job description or income level or color of skin or nationality, but life itself and the relationships that nurture life. Often, the mourning process does that; it makes us more aware of precious relationships and the sacredness of life.

They shall be comforted.

Most of us know the experience of mourning and of accompanying others who mourn, but rarely do we think of being *called* to mourn, an intensely personal and painful part of life's journey. The loss of loved ones brings us face to face with our most deeply held beliefs, whether their death is sudden, expected, preventable.

When my mother died, one of my daughters wrote to her friends: "My beloved Grand died this evening just a few weeks short of her 95th birthday. *Allah yir-hamaha.* (May she rest in peace.) She lived a long and fortunate life and died peacefully. May all people on earth someday be so fortunate."

"May all people on earth someday be so fortunate." Surely a vocation shaped by this beatitude would be striving to make that vision a reality.

But two other particular dimensions of this vocation strike me as enormously important as well. They are *social comforting* and *earth mourning.*

Social Comforting

By "social comforting" I mean the vocation to accompany people who are in mourning as a result of war, political violence, social injustice, natural disasters, when the suffering assumes a scale so huge that the pain individuals or families suffer is subsumed into the wailing of a whole community, a whole country, an entire racial or cultural group.

The events of 9/11 were a good example, and the instinctive response of most people was exactly what I mean by social comforting. The outpouring of care and concern for those who lost loved ones in the World Trade Center or the Pentagon was immediate and heartfelt.

The nationwide, worldwide responses to the murders of Amish school children in October 2006 and to the unthinkable, senseless violence at Virginia Tech in April 2007 were others.

Another was the call, the vocation we all heard to provide humanitarian assistance when South Asian coastal areas were devastated by the tsunami, or when Pakistan was reeling from a devastating earthquake.

A vocation to social comforting was also heard by many people and communities when Hurricane Katrina struck New Orleans and the Gulf Coast. But that call went far beyond the provision of emergency humanitarian aid because Hurricane

Katrina laid bare a shocking level of poverty and racial injustice. This vocation included an invitation to address root causes in the United States of deep social ills.

Social comforting moves us to uproot social injustice.

To respond with compassion to the suffering of slaves required the uprooting of slavery. To respond with compassion to the suffering of people of African descent or immigrants in the United States or elsewhere will require the uprooting of racism.

During the wars and repression in Central America in the 1980s, thousands of U.S. people, many of them people of faith, found themselves responding in the affirmative to an invitation to accompany people brutalized by governments supported by the United States. They met people like Rufina Amaya, who was the sole survivor of a 1981 massacre at El Mozote in El Salvador. Hundreds of people were slaughtered by the Salvadoran military in that small village on December 11, including Rufina's husband and all her children. Suffering like hers was evident all over the region, as it was in Rwanda, is now in Darfur, and has been in too many corners of the world.

A vocation that accompanies this intensity of social pain will respond to the specific needs of individuals like Rufina, but also will work furiously to ensure the dismantling of systems of repression so that such tragedies will never be repeated.

Throughout the years of the sanctions in Iraq and as the U.S. war there became a certainty, courageous people from around the world, members of organizations like Voices in the Wilderness[32] and the Christian Peacemaker Teams,[33] spent more time in Baghdad, comforting those whose lives were devastated by the sanctions and who were terrified by the prospect of war. As part of their vocation to social comforting, and because they saw with their own eyes the cost of war to everyone it touched, these holy people came home and worked unrelentingly to end the war.

Many people from around the world, including staff of Catholic Relief Services,[34] were drawn to Rwanda after the genocide; to Colombia caught in brutal civil war for decades; to East Timor during and after their hard won independence. Their vocation to comfort those who mourn also led them to the work of peace-building and social justice.

Blessed are those who mourn.

Earth Mourning

And blessed are those who mourn for the earth.

Millions of people in our world feel in their souls a deep and painful rupture in a relationship with the earth that once was personal and vital — every drop of water carried and counted, every stalk of corn blessed. Forced to pull up roots from a place where that relationship was nurtured, they have moved on, escaping war, poverty, emptiness, and even progress, in search of survival. Many are driven to migrate by distant, powerful forces in the global economy; others, by drought or deliberate policies of displacement; yet others by violence or racism or the empty promises of a consumer paradise. In all cases, fundamental relationships between people and creation have been damaged or destroyed.

Other millions, especially those in the so-called "developed" world, have never known the earth as anything other than a place to dump their garbage and bury their dead. Their alienation is profound. They think that food comes wrapped in plastic, coated with wax, or enclosed in a box. They have no idea where water comes from, except from a tap, and they assume it will always be there, hot and cold and potable, even if someone has to steal it for them.

Whether through the unceasing, enormous demands of consumer societies, the desperation of indebted, impoverished economies, or the devastation of war, the earth is threatened as never before. Theologian Larry Rasmussen writes about how holes in the ozone layer, clear-cut forests, drained wetlands, denuded grasslands and soils, polluted air, rivers, and coastal waters, poisoned oceans, disrupted habitats and completely unmanageable wastes, especially nuclear wastes, make that clear.[35] How much of the earth's surface has been rendered untouchable by the planting of landmines rather than productive by the planting of life-giving crops? How many neighborhoods and villages have become unlivable due to toxic waste?

Like all mourning, *earth mourning* also responds to death, to loss, to the destruction of the earth community of which every human being is a part.

Sister Dorothy Stang, a sister of Notre Dame de Namur from Ohio, heard and responded to this vocation and ultimately gave her life for it. Her life as a missionary in Brazil was totally given to building right relationships within the community of all life.

She made real in Pará, the part of Brazil where she lived and worked, the connection between the dignity of the individual and the need to construct just societies. She, like thousands of other pastoral agents and communities, understood the need for consonance between what we say we believe and how we live, between our personal journeys in faith and Jesus' invitation to follow him.

But slowly, slowly in recent years a new movement of the Spirit began to bear fruit in her as well. One turning point for Dorothy was the Earth Summit, which she attended in Rio de Janeiro.

Taking place in June 1992, the United Nations Conference on Environment and Development, or Earth Summit, attracted over thirty thousand people including more than a hundred heads of state. For the first time, the attention of the world was fixed on the need to address the serious and sometimes irreversible damage being done by human beings to the rest of creation.

Theologians and ethicists, scientists and environmental activists had been opening this door for many years prior to 1992. Theologian Thomas Berry had already presented us with a challenge to understand in new ways our location in relation to the cosmos. In much the same way the church in Latin America, and we, were challenged to understand our relationships with marginalized and oppressed peoples, not as a dominant species exploiting the rest of creation for our own benefit, but as part of the community of all life.

Slowly this new movement of the Spirit helped us understand that the dignity of the person and the survival of the planet are intrinsically interconnected.

People close to the land and indigenous peoples seem to see this clearly, that the same systems and structures and patterns of human life that destroy individuals and the human community are destroying the earth. Dorothy saw it too and acted accordingly, integrating an option for the earth with her option for the poor.

Maryknoll missioners living in the rain forest of Panama, in the mountains of the Philippines, in the growing deserts of Oaxaca, Mexico, or East Africa, in small island states threatened by rising waters did likewise.

A new cosmovision, a new sense of the inherent dignity and worth of all creation, a new reading of the sacred text and the Christian tradition began to take place. Catholic social teaching began to include a call to respect the integrity of creation.

People began to realize that the earth and its bounty are not commodities for human consumption, but that they have rights of their own. We began to mourn for the dying earth. We began to absorb a sense of the gratuitousness and wonder of creation, to retell the story of creation, the story of the Garden of Eden, to redefine movement toward the New Creation as the restoration of right relationships between human beings and with all of the created order.

In February 2005 Dorothy Stang was murdered. She gave her life for something she believed in very deeply. Dorothy claimed and lived the fullness of life with the human communities of which she was a part and with the earth community she learned to love so well. As a result of her social mourning she demanded that the poor people of Pará be treated with justice. As a result of her earth mourning, she demanded that the rest of creation be treated justly as well. Powerful interests bent on exploiting human labor and consuming the earth were threatened by both and did away with her. Her life sang with the Preamble to the Earth Charter:

> We stand at a critical moment in Earth's history, a time when humanity must choose its future. As the world becomes increasingly interdependent and fragile, the future at once holds great peril and great promise. To move forward we must recognize that in the midst of a magnificent diversity of cultures and life forms we are one human family and one Earth community with a common destiny. We must join together to bring forth a sustainable global society founded on respect for nature, universal human rights, economic justice, and a culture of peace. Towards this end, it is imperative that we, the peoples of Earth, declare our responsibility to one another, to the greater community of life, and to future generations.[36]

Work for Justice and Participation in the Transformation of the World

Blessed are they who hunger and thirst for righteousness [justice], for they will be filled.... Blessed are they who are persecuted for righteousness' [justice'] sake, for theirs is the kingdom of heaven.

If we take seriously the vocation to become poor or poor in spirit, if we take seriously the vocation to mourn, we will understand more clearly the vocation to *hunger and thirst for justice.*

One essential dimension of the life and ministry of Jesus was his commitment to creating a just and inclusive community. He deliberately moved to the margins to embrace the excluded. He evaluated social structures in first-century Palestine from the perspective of the excluded. And he acted to change the structures — structures that *applied* the Roman occupation, structures that *sustained* the privileges of the Judean ruling class, structures that excluded the lepers, the women, the others called "unclean" — with such dedication that it got him killed. His vision was of an inclusive community. He set out to make it real, and he invited us, *called* us, to follow him.

Today, the encounter with structural evil or sin continues on a grand scale. What we can see by accompanying those who are poor, by becoming poor in spirit, what we see when we mourn and comfort others who mourn, what we see when we mourn for the earth is sometimes the fruit of ignorance or natural disaster. But very often the poverty and brokenness we see is the result of deeply institutionalized evil — social sin: the unjust ownership of and access to productive land and other resources, regressive tax laws, exclusionary zoning regulations, unjust migration and immigration laws, little or inadequate access to education and health care, illegitimate debt, unjust trade regulations, unregulated and exploitative activities of transnational corporations and banks — and on and on.

Into this milieu we are called, we are given a vocation, to bring the Good News, first and foremost by Jesus' example. "Follow me."

Some of us spend our work lives or significant volunteer time promoting social justice. We work for diocesan social ministry offices, parishes, Catholic Charities,[37] Catholic Relief Services, NETWORK: A National Catholic Social Justice Lobby,[38] the Center of Concern,[39] Bread for the World.[40] We represent religious communities at the United Nations in New York or Geneva. We advocate for economic justice at the World Bank, the International Monetary Fund, the World Trade Organization. We do research and analysis; we try to create space at decision-making tables for people to advocate for their own rights; we organize and we advocate.

We live one expression of the vocation to do justice. But I believe there is a more important expression of this vocation that should take root in the life of every follower of Jesus.

Over the twenty plus years of Assisi Community's existence, in addition to the men and women religious I introduced earlier in this book, we have counted among our members lay people from many different walks of life: professional musicians, lawyers, teachers, authors, a press secretary for a member of Congress, a medical doctor, someone working for a U.S. government agency, people working for nonprofit community-based organizations serving homeless people and immigrants, theologians, a physicist, child- and elder-care givers, religious educators, service workers, an accountant, caterers, a nurse, students, a chef, an investment broker, and computer experts. All were committed to integrating work for social justice into their personal and work lives. The necessary ingredients were community and creativity.

The role of community, it seems to me, is to provide both discernment and support, as well as to challenge each of us to live the gospel in our own lives. And creativity is a priceless treasure, a gift of the Holy Spirit, I think, that helps us imagine new forms of discipleship and try them out, one step at a time.

This vocation to do justice is not an easy one, but it is very well rooted in the Scriptures and our tradition. Catholic social teaching, for example, provides a deep and rich theological basis for the vocation of evangelizing the social, cultural, economic, political, and military structures of our times. It is a clear and unambiguous expression of the gospel's call to the community of disciples to work for social justice.

From the beginning,[41] Catholic social teaching recognized that the way societies were organizing relationships and the balance of power, for example, between labor and capital, between the state and the private sector, between personal rights and social responsibilities had moral implications. The *structures* of society, in addition to the moral character and behavior of *individuals,* were to be evaluated according to gospel criteria and called to account.

In the first seventy years or so of Catholic social teaching, the pace of evaluation and proclamation by the official church was slow, but the content was extremely important. *That* the church had something to say about the way the world was put together in the late nineteenth and the first half of the twentieth centuries was important *then; what* it said then, which was rooted in an absolute belief in the inherent dignity of each person, *remains absolutely crucial* today.

In *Catholic Social Teaching: Our Best Kept Secret,* Edward DeBerri and James Hug note that in our tradition the great commandment to love one's neighbor is an absolute demand for justice; charity or love *has to manifest itself* in actions and structures that promote human dignity, protect human rights, and facilitate human development.[42] To promote justice is to transform the structures that block love. To love each and every person requires that we work to establish structures of justice that support and liberate all peoples. In a world shaped by complex systems of global interaction, just structures to give form to that interaction are called by Pope Paul VI "love's minimum expression."

A vocation to do justice *is,* but *is not only,* a call to right interpersonal relationships; it is also a call to right social relationships, to socially just systems and structures.

In the years during and after the Second Vatican Council, with *Gaudium et Spes* and a rapid succession of other documents, the Catholic Church became fully engaged in the modern (and postmodern) world, calling for social and economic justice, solidarity, peace and the "evangelization of structures and cultures."

More and more clearly the task of evangelizing the structures of the world was defined. In 1971 the Synod of Bishops wrote in *Justice in the World:* "Action on behalf of justice and participation in the transformation of the world fully appear to us as a constitutive dimension of the preaching of the Gospel, or in other words, of the church's mission for the redemption of the human race and its liberation from every oppressive situation."[43]

In the last half of the twentieth century, Catholic social teaching called all the people of God to "read the signs of the times" and to respond as the gospel would demand. On the eightieth anniversary of *Rerum Novarum,* Paul VI wrote: "It is up to the Christian communities to analyze with objectivity the situation which is proper to their own country, to shed on it the light of the Gospel's unalterable words and to draw principles of reflection, norms of judgment and directives for action from the social teaching of the Church."[44]

The norms of judgment and directives for action from the social teaching of the church, the well-articulated theological base from which we engage the structures and systems of our world, serve us pretty well as we try to figure out what it means to have a *vocation* to promote social justice.

At a personal level, in our families, work life, neighborhoods, cities, in our parishes, dioceses, and the universal church, as a country, in domestic and foreign policy and practice, and globally, in the myriad ways we craft and recraft the shape of international relations, we are constantly called to apply the principles of Catholic social teaching:

- the dignity of the human person;
- the dignity of work by which persons express and develop being;
- the call to community, to right relationships with other people;
- human rights (social and economic as well as civil and political) that imply extensive responsibilities;
- option for the poor;
- solidarity;
- care for creation, the call to right relationships with the whole community of life.

Peacemaking and Reconciliation

In my work with Maryknoll and Pax Christi International,[45] a worldwide Catholic movement for peace and reconciliation, I interact very often with people living with and responding to violent conflict and its aftermath — from the Democratic Republic of the Congo to the Philippines, from El Salvador to East Timor, Croatia to Cambodia, Guatemala to the Sudan, Colombia, Iraq, and Afghanistan. I have reflected often on the vocation to peacemaking, peace-building, and have learned at the feet of many people called to this vocation. In the U.S. Catholic community, I think in particular of the following, to name a few:

- the communion of saints around Pax Christi USA[46] and the Catholic Worker movement;

- M.J. and Jerry Park and their Little Friends for Peace,[47] which has introduced thousands of schoolchildren to conflict resolution skills at elementary schools, parishes, and summer camps;

- Jim and Kathleen McGinnis and their Institute for Peace and Justice[48] with its Parenting for Peace and Justice Network, Families Against Violence Advocacy Network, Teens Acting for Peace, and other programs;

- the Franciscans and their friends who founded and developed Pace e Bene Nonviolence Service,[49] which helps people and communities build skills for nonviolent living through their programs, including "From Violence to Wholeness" and "Engage";

- the academics, clergy and lay people of the Catholic Peacebuilding Network,[50] which seeks to enhance the study and practice of Catholic peace-building, especially at the local level.

Faith grounds and shapes the work of all of these groups and so many others with a vocation to work for peace. As they teach alternatives to violence at home and in our neighborhoods, as they accompany communities torn apart by violence, as they work to prevent or stop war, eliminate trafficking in small arms, ban the use of landmines and cluster bombs, end the production and stockpiling of weapons of mass destruction, shift budget priorities from preparations for war to support for life, eliminate the roots of war, promote reconciliation at home and in the world, Jesus' Sermon on the Mount is the guidebook they try to follow.

It calls us to accompany people who are threatened by violence and to nurture relationships across boundaries, real or fabricated. It calls us to apply consistently a moral framework as we face the possibility of violent conflict or war. And it calls us to pray for reconciliation and lasting peace.

Like other vocations, the contours of a peacemaking vocation are made more visible by the practice of accompaniment, being with people who are threatened by potential violence or who are living with one or another form of violence on a regular basis.

The most significant peacemaking role Maryknoll missioners play is that of neighbor in communities struggling for survival and peace. Theirs is a long-term presence, often for twenty or thirty years or more, giving witness to the great value they place on the people, their community, and their culture. By their presence they plant deep and lasting roots of peace.

A similar peacemaking vocation is lived in a powerful and prophetic way by Christian Peacemaker Teams in Israel and Palestine, Colombia, and along the U.S.-Mexico border; the Ecumenical Accompaniment Project[51] in Israel and Palestine; Witness for Peace[52] in Mexico, Guatemala, and Colombia and many others like them, who provide a measure of safety for people living in particularly dangerous situations, most often in the context of violent conflict or war.

Those who answer the call to be peacemakers now will walk on yet unknown pathways and create a new framework for applying the tenets of our faith tradition in our profoundly un-peaceful world.

I believe that such a framework should be shaped by the experience of communities devastated by violent conflict. They know in their souls the consequences of war, even of wars that were considered "just."

Salvadoran theologian Jon Sobrino, S.J., has witnessed all the horror and destruction of repression, of a war to stop the repression, of street violence in the aftermath of war, and of unsolved social and economic inequities. Six of his Jesuit brothers were killed during El Salvador's brutal civil war: Ignacio Ellacuría, rector of the Jesuit university in San Salvador; Segundo Montes, sociologist; Ignacio Martín-Baró, social psychologist; Juan Ramón Moreno, professor of theology; Amando López, professor of theology; and Joaquín López y López, founder of the university.

Their blood and the blood of all the martyrs of El Salvador, known and unknown, was spilled for a just peace that has not yet arrived. Jon Sobrino and survivors of the war in El Salvador should help shape this new moral framework. So should other grassroots communities around the world that have learned lessons about war and peace from personal experience.

Those who answer the call to be peacemakers now will walk on yet unknown pathways and create a new framework for applying the tenets of our faith tradition in our profoundly un-peaceful world.

Katarina Kruhonja is a medical doctor from Osijek, Croatia, where she co-founded the Center for Peace, Nonviolence, and Human Rights in 1992 in the middle of war in the former Yugoslavia. At first, the only peacemaking possible was to witness against war and to provide support for refugees and displaced people, but slowly Katarina and her peacemaking colleagues began to network with groups opposed to war on the Serbian side of the conflict and to bring people together in neutral locations. As the region began to make a transition to peace, they, with perhaps a hundred other peace activists, went village to village and house to house preparing for the reintegration of recently fighting communities and, as the reintegration progressed, they helped people come together across ethnic lines to dialogue about the future. Now, slowly, they are beginning to help people deal with the painful past. Katarina has seen the ravages of war too many times to think of war as a solution. She and her colleagues at the Center for Peace, Nonviolence, and Human Rights should help articulate this new moral framework.

From communities like these that have been immersed in violence, clear lessons about peace have begun to emerge:

- Every human life is sacred without exception; the children of Afghanistan or Iraq are as precious in the eyes of God as the lives of my grandchildren.

- Extreme care has to be taken to understand and honor the rich cultural differences that exist between peoples; cross-cultural and interfaith dialogue are extremely important peacebuilding tools.

- There are no short-term solutions to violence at any level; lasting peace will only be discovered when we address the deep roots of violence.

- War or any response to violence with more violence will never achieve peace.

- Peacemaking is an essential component of the Christian vocation.

The Beatitudes lead us beyond platitudes about peace-making to a vocation that is clear and very challenging, personally and interpersonally, in our communities, at work, as citizens of our nation, and as members of the global community.

The Pax Christi litany of peacemakers reminds us of the rich peacemaking tradition that is ours:

God, creator of the universe, author of our covenant of peace, *we pray to you, empower us to be peacemakers!*

God, redeemer of the world, our way of peace . . .

God, sanctifier of conscience, gift of peace . . .

Mary, wellspring of reconciliation, mother of peace-makers . . .

Michael, our defender in the spiritual battle with forces of our own self-destruction . . .

Heavenly hosts, angelic warriors for universal peace . . .

Moses and Miriam, nonviolent liberators, architects and singers of the covenant of justice . . .

Isaiah, critic of militarism, prophet of peace . . .

Esther, intercessor for the powerless, emissary of peace . . .

Amos and Micah and Hosea, voices for the oppressed . . .

Jeremiah, doomsday seer, voice of lamentation . . .

Magdalene, faithful witness of Christ's execution, first witness of his resurrection . . .

Peter and Paul, prisoners of conscience . . .

Matthew, Mark, Luke, John, evangelists of the peaceable Reign of God . . .

Felicity and Perpetua, midwives and mothers, sacrificed in the sport of a military empire . . .

Martin of Tours, conscientious objector . . .

Francis of Assisi, lover of creation, poor man with nothing to fight for ...

Clare of Assisi, pacifier of armies with the power of the Eucharist ...

Catherine of Siena, mystic diplomat, skilled negotiator ...

Hildegarde of Bingen, mystic, lover of creation ...

Gandhi, the Mahatma, nonviolent warrior ...

Franz Jägerstätter resister for Christ ...

Simone Weil, patroness of solidarity with the oppressed, fasting unto death with the hungry ...

Martin Luther King Jr., prophet and dreamer of the Beloved Community ...

Thomas Merton, contemplative critic, mentor of peacemakers ...

Pope John XXIII, herald of peace ...

Pope Paul VI, apostle and teacher of peace ...

Dorothy Day, lady poverty, mother of courage, witness to the radical gospel of peace ...

Oscar Romero, shepherd of the poor, martyr for justice ...

Maura, Ita, Jean, Dorothy, martyrs for the poor, handmaids of justice ...

Saints of the Shaker, Mennonite, Quaker, and Church of the Brethren communions ...

Children of light, transfigured in the firestorms of
  Hiroshima and Nagasaki...

Children of darkness, transfigured in the night of torture
  and disappearance...

All you holy peacemakers, living and more living...

Jesus, Messiah, Prince of Peace...[53]

The vocation to peacemaking, one specifically identified by
Jesus in the Sermon on the Mount, is a call to all of us to
live peace, to learn how to resolve conflicts without resort to
violence, and to reconcile a broken world wherever we find
ourselves day by day. In other words, the vocation to peacemaking has to permeate our lives and infuse our worldview.
The pursuit of peace, which is the absence of war and much
more than the absence of war, must become the Christian's
constant companion, whatever other occupation or state in
life we might pursue.

*Blessed are the peacemakers, for they shall be called
children of God.*

Chapter Four

Called to the Fullness of Life

Rejoice and leap for joy on that day! For your reward will be great in heaven. (Matthew 5:12)

The Beatitudes...shed light on the actions and attitudes characteristic of the Christian life; they are the paradoxical promises that sustain hope in the midst of tribulations; they proclaim the blessings and rewards already secured, however dimly, for Christ's disciples.[54]

DAY AFTER DAY we are inundated with bad news from around the world. We see a human community devastated by poverty and war, by violences of every imaginable shape and intensity, by greed and corruption. We see that the rest of creation is under unrelenting assault that may soon render our beautiful planet uninhabitable. We see threats that were almost unthinkable a few decades ago: the HIV/AIDS pandemic, seemingly incurable poverty, terrorism, wars in response to terrorism, climate change and global warming, environmental racism, forced and massive migrations, torture, trafficking in drugs and weapons and people, overdevelopment, extreme concentrations of wealth and power, private control for profit of basic resources like water, wanton disregard for the sanctity of life. The list, sadly, is very long and we know it well.

But when we look around, we also see a world of amazing hope and creative energy for change, a world rising up for justice. And *that* is where any reflection on vocation ultimately must go.

> *Right next to the devastated land-scape of an impoverished, violent, unjust, and damaged world some sturdy little flowers continue to sprout. They enable us day after day, year after year, in an increasingly bleak world, to give an accounting of our hope.*

One of my favorite passages in Scripture is from Peter's first epistle (3:15): "Always be ready to make your defense to anyone who demands from you an accounting for the hope that is in you." I like this passage because Peter simply *assumes* that those who follow Jesus *will* have hope. It is in fact one of the defining characteristics of the Christian community. We are Resurrection people; we are *hopers*. But for the vast majority of people in our world whose lives are immersed in a tragic contemporary reality, who live face to face with evil and its consequences or with horrendous suffering, it is a very challenging passage. And for those of us who *choose* to open our eyes and our hearts to the human face of injustice or oppression, or to a devastated earth, it is also a very challenging passage. Is it possible for us to give an accounting for our hope? And how is hope tied to happiness?

Theologian Jon Sobrino, S.J., writes that his brothers, the Jesuit martyrs of El Salvador, were filled with joy. From the standpoint of the Beatitudes and at the level of life's meaning, they were deeply happy.

> By carrying out their work from the standpoint and for the sake of the poor, they participated in their reality, which gave them a fundamental human dignity and filled them with joy....
>
> By letting themselves be enlightened by the poor and see the world through purified eyes, they experienced the joy of holding the truth and serving the truth....
>
> By living and dying for justice for the poor, they found a superior food, one which satisfies the hunger of humanity and fraternity....
>
> By working to achieve peace amidst repression and war, even if they themselves were repressed, defaced, and slandered, they achieved true peace,...upon which they could rest their hearts....
>
> By stepping into conflicts and remaining with them until the end, until giving their own lives, they achieved the maximum joy, which is the maximum paradox. By giving their lives, they showed the greatest love, and that made them live.[55]

These men had answered a call. Actually, they had answered many calls. They were Jesuits, scholars, teachers, and researchers. They were pastors. They had moved themselves to the side of El Salvador's poor majority both personally and professionally.

They were killed because, like Jesus, the enormously positive qualities that defined their lives made them unbearable threats to those in power. In living their lives for justice' sake, they found life and happiness even in the midst of terrible violence and danger. In giving their lives for justice' sake, they entered, we believe, the fullness of life and joy.

Announcing the Good News

To retell the story of these men is to announce the Good News.

The mandate of the Maryknoll Office for Global Concerns is to work for "peace, social justice, and the integrity of creation." Often we find ourselves *denouncing* rather than *announcing,* holding on to hope that is admittedly thin: hope that we can stop torture, eradicate poverty, end wars — at least *this* war or *that* war — reverse climate change, eliminate weapons of mass destruction and terrorism and racism. Unfortunately, I think we will always have to be about the task of denouncing, of stopping, of reversing.

That is part of the vocation of privileged people in an impoverished world, of peaceful people in a world of random and not-so-random violence, of secure people in a threatened world, of over-consuming people in a world of limited resources. But that is not our main vocation. There is an announcing side to this mandate as well.

Right next to the devastated landscape of an impoverished, violent, unjust, and damaged world some sturdy little flowers continue to sprout. They enable us day after day, year after year, in an increasingly bleak world, to give an accounting of our hope.

Close to home we see them clearly: our children, their children, our students and young friends who are searching through all the distractions and temptations and fears of youth to identify and start down their own "right" pathway toward a meaningful life; wise and faithful "elders" in all our communities who live the gospel fully and with passion; servant leaders in our places of work, our parishes, our neighborhoods, our cities and towns, our country who dedicate themselves in hundreds of different ways to the common good; and the prophets among us who make us uncomfortably aware of the distance we have yet to go before we are who we are called to be.

The flowers we encounter in this broken world are often small, but they are of many different colors and varieties, and they are beautiful, each one. They are sprouting vigorously as more people come to believe that another world is possible and are giving their lives, living out their vocations, to make the "other world" a reality.

We are clearer than we have ever been before that justice for human beings and justice for the rest of creation, including the earth herself, are intrinsically interconnected. We are clearer than ever before that without social justice there will be no peace and that without peace there will be no social justice. We know that the roots of the flowers are woven together. They will thrive only in the soil of global solidarity, nourished by a faith that calls us to account for the hope that is in us.

Our task is to see these flowers sprouting, to celebrate them and to help them grow.

Václav Havel was a playwright and dissident in Communist Czechoslovakia. He was a founding member of Charter 77, the small group of dissidents demanding basic human rights from their government. He ultimately became the president of the Czech Republic. In an essay that he published in 1978, Havel wrote about "living in truth," doing what you think needs to be done and saying what you understand to be a truth that needs saying. He deeply believed that to live in the truth was to be powerful and he was right. In Czechoslovakia and Poland, for example, people who had no basic freedoms under Soviet communism began to live in the truth. To act "as if" they had freedom of assembly, they simply began to assemble; to act "as if" they had freedom of expression, they simply began to speak truth; to act "as if" they had freedom of the press, they simply began to publish.

The Beatitudes call us to do the same: to live as if our value as human beings were not limited to how much we can produce or consume; to live as if we were not constantly prodded to buy products we do not need and cannot afford; to live as if we cared deeply about the rest of the world.

By living "as if" we announce the in-breaking of the Reign of God.

Both Matthew and Luke follow the Beatitudes immediately with explicit instructions for the followers of Jesus that describe quite well how we might, in these times, live "as if." To live according to their instructions would distinguish us from the mainstream of Western culture as clearly as Gandhi and Havel and Lech Walesa and Jesus stood out from the mainstream in their times:

- To the person who strikes you on one cheek, offer the other one as well, and from the person who takes your cloak, do not withhold even your shirt. (Luke 6: 29)

- Give to everyone who asks of you, and from the one who takes what is yours do not demand it back. (Luke 6:30)

- Love your enemies and pray for those who persecute you. (Matt. 5:44)

- Do not store up for yourselves treasures on earth, where moth and rust consume and where thieves break in and steal, but store up for yourselves treasures in heaven, where neither moth nor rust consumes and where thieves do not break in and steal. For where your treasure is, there your heart will be also. (Matt. 6:19–21)

- Do to others what you would have them do to you. (Matt. 7:12; Luke 6: 30)

And if we try to follow this vocation to the Christian life, in the very same sermon, Jesus said:

- Give and gifts will be given to you; a good measure, packed together, shaken down, and overflowing, will be poured into your lap. For the measure with which you measure will in return be measured out to you. (Luke 6:38)

The beatitude we are promised...teaches us that true happiness is not found in riches or well-being, in human fame or power, or in any human achievement — however beneficial it may be..., but in God alone, the source of every good and of all love.[56]

The Beatitudes...proclaim the blessings and rewards already secured, however dimly, for Christ's disciples.[57]

Meaning, Joy, Fullness of Life

Increasingly I am convinced that as adults and honest followers of Christ we know in our souls when we are living faithfully the vocation or vocations to which we have been called. We know Jesus' story very well. We know what and how he called all of us to be and we know when we have followed and when we have turned away in sadness like the rich young man.

If we look very carefully at the reality of the world into which we are sent — with all its hopes and fears, joys and sorrows, which, if we are open to them, soon become our own — then we will begin to *hear* the Good News. If we have the courage to ask why the brokenness we see is so pervasive, why the beauty is so rarely seen, then we will begin to *hear* the Good News. If we have readied ourselves to be changed, converted, to find God as we are called and respond to new vocations, then we will begin to *hear* the Good News. It will begin to make sense to us in ways we never thought possible; we will see it lived in three dimensions and in brilliant color.

To our vocations, our journeys, our lives we also hopefully will *bring and be* the Good News, wherever we are. During the twenty-fifth anniversary celebration of the martyrdom of the four U.S. churchwomen killed in El Salvador, Jesuit theologian Jon Sobrino said that these women, Jean, Ita, Maura, and Dorothy, brought love, decency, solidarity, joy, and hope to El Salvador in those years — the Good News — and that when they were killed he began to realize in a new way the extent of the evil with which the people, especially the poor, in El Salvador were contending.

As we live out our vocations in the coming years, we will *encounter* and *bring* and *be* the Good News, but we will do so in an ever-new and deeply challenging global reality.

The world into which we are called is rapidly integrating. The gap between those who have and those who do not is huge, and showing itself in dramatic ways, separating those who survive treatable diseases from those who do not; those who have assured access to essential medicines from those who do not; those who are always and profoundly vulnerable to natural disasters from those who have access to safer space; those who work the land from those who own the land; those who wash their floors with potable water from those who know too well the terror of dry wells and soaring water prices; those who eat too much from those who never have enough.

In that world, this world, we human beings are just beginning to understand ourselves as part of the community of all life, and few of us are yet willing to accept the implications of that on a daily basis.

As we accompany the pain and celebrate the beauty wherever we are planted, as we nurture just relationships and live compassionate lives, we are, we will be, helping to build the beloved global community of all life.

The Beatitudes respond to the natural desire for happiness. This desire is of divine origin: God has placed it in the human heart in order to draw man to the One who alone can fulfill it.[58]

The New Creation and the Tree of Life

Larry Rasmussen notes that the Hebrew Bible begins with the tree of life ("Out of the ground the Lord God made to grow every tree that is pleasant to the sight and good for food, the tree of life also in the midst of the garden," Gen. 2:9) and that the Christian Bible ends with the tree of life ("On either side of the river is the tree of life with its twelve kinds of fruit, producing its fruit each month; and the leaves of the tree are for the healing of the nations," Rev. 22:1–2).[59]

Rasmussen writes about the tree of life as a rich symbol with deep meaning in many different cultures across Africa, the Americas, and around the world. He describes the tree of life as it is carved by peoples of Mexican and Native American ancestry living along the Mexico-U.S. border as "a colorfully crowded cottonwood with fruits, flowers, birds and people — signs of life on every branch." In other cultures, trees have been the dwelling place of divinities; the roots of trees have gently encompassed the earth, holding it together; trees have been a metaphor for fidelity and righteousness, healing and new life; and trees have been a strong symbol of resistance — from trees planted by Nelson Mandela when he was imprisoned on Robben Island to the tree that grew in Brooklyn.

Each Spring, not far from where I live, the most spectacular display of beauty presents itself. A very old white dogwood tree stretches out its majestic branches with an Alleluia! that echoes the song of Resurrection; our communities are always singing as this beautiful tree wakens from its winter slumber. It is by far the largest dogwood tree I have ever seen. In its branches for weeks you can hear the songs of birds and the chatter of the squirrels that make it their home. In the fall its generous red berries, inedible to humans, provide a sumptuous feast for other creatures. And its red leaves in the fall are a beautiful auger of the approaching cold.

As the time approaches each year for the flowering of the dogwood in Washington, DC, my heart begins to rise, and when this beautiful old friend bursts into bloom, I am filled with delight, a glimmer of the "not yet."

> The beatitude we are promised...teaches us that true happiness is not found in riches or well-being, in human fame or power, or in any human achievement — however beneficial it may be..., but in God alone, the source of every good and of all love.[60]

On the other side of the world in Tanzania there stands another tree, a particular baobab tree whose picture I took a few years ago. Also beautiful, this majestic tree towers over the spectacular landscape of the Tarangire National Park, providing shade, shelter, or food for elephant families and giraffes and baboons and birds and dozens of God's other creatures passing through toward water or staying for a bit of respite from the sun. For humans it provides fruit and bark for baskets and roots for medicine. The baobab is considered a sacred tree.

Like the Mexican and Native American tree of life, it is filled to the brim with creation, alive and thriving and living in harmony.

That is what we are promised if we answer the call.

Listen! Catch the rhythm of God's voice. Sometimes we hear it deep in our own souls; at other times, through a dialogue of the heart with another person; or through discernment in community; or in something we read or observe about the earth herself or events in the world.

The fulfillment of vocation is celebration of life in God (*Blessed are you.... Happy are you...*), celebration that *is* life in God, the paradoxical promises, the blessings and rewards, the already and the not yet.[61]

Epilogue

S O WE END where we began, asking "What am I called to do for the rest of my life?" Discerning your vocation is a lifelong process of learning to follow Jesus. What is your next right step? What are you called to do to be a faithful disciple in these times, in this world? Who and how are you called to be *now?*

You have probably already said yes to God's call, maybe many times over in your twenty or thirty or fifty or more years. Perhaps you are well settled into God's niche for you. But you will know in your heart when the space opens in your life to listen again for new direction. You will feel the gentle or not-so-gentle prodding of the Spirit. You will find yourself listening again for the rhythm of God's voice.

Vocation is lived in a wide variety of ways; there are many different pathways even in one faithful life.

Yet you know how easy it is to settle into life, to stop listening for that still small voice. The busy-ness of your daily activities consumes your time and attention. You run from one serious responsibility to another, one important event to another. Your mind is full of plans and concerns. You live with "surround-sound" and unrelenting instantaneous communication.

Stop. Create the space to listen. Allow yourself the time to hear what God is saying in your life. Be still enough to see, really see, what is going on in the world and to ask how you might respond, how you might participate in the healing of the world, and thereby your own healing.

Believe that yours is a call to the fullness of life. Allow that reality to infuse every corner of your being: your spirituality, your values, what you care about, how you use your time and resources, your relationships, your work.

> *Think of all the places where you might hear God's voice more clearly and make sure you go there regularly.*

No matter where you are or what your calling, try to deepen your reflections on your vocation. Pray for the guidance of the Spirit. Fill the canvas of your life with new possibilities. Enrich what you are already doing by making it conform more intentionally to the gospel. Shape your decisions about life more deliberately by a commitment to the New Creation.

Remember that you can discover a new vocation at any time of your life. You can respond to more than one call at a time. Vocation is about the totality of how we live the gospel in these times.

Think of all the places where you might hear God's voice more clearly and make sure you go there regularly.

Our God is full of surprises. Over and over again, she invites us to follow in ways that we don't expect or understand into places we had not planned to go. We have many opportunities to catch the cadence of her voice.

Look very carefully at the reality of the world into which we are sent, with all its hopes and fears, joys and sorrows, which, if you are open to them, will soon become your own. Have the courage to ask why the brokenness you see is so pervasive, why the beauty is so rarely seen. Ready yourself to be changed, converted, to find God as you are called and respond to new vocations. You will begin to recognize the cadence of God's call and it will begin to make sense to you in ways you never thought possible.

Open yourself to a dialogue of the heart with those who are hurting or marginalized, violated or forgotten. The reality they live may help you hear God more clearly or give you the courage to respond. A Christian vocation will often lead us to the margins: "Whatsoever you do to the least of these. . . . " But what to do when we get there can be the question. Listen there to the inner voice. Ask how you can be present to those who are hurt or forgotten. Integrate a response to their needs and work for social justice with them or on their behalf in what you are already doing or what you are called now to do. How will your next steps make their next steps easier, less painful, less frustrating?

Discern in community God's call for you. Remember always that you live in a global community, but also be or become part of a community closer to home, a community that shares your faith and values. Whether your primary community is your family or your parish or a circle of friends or an intentional community that lives together, sharing life day by day, or a worshiping community that journeys together from a bit more distance, lean on your community as you listen for God's call.

Tune your soul also to God's song in creation. The groaning of creation in our times is in tune with the rhythm of God's call. Listening to the cry of the earth sharpens our capacity to hear God's voice. Allow the harmony you begin to discern in creation to open your heart to new challenges in life.

You know in your soul whether or not you are living faithfully the vocation or vocations to which you have been called. Take the next right step. God is calling — through loved ones and community, through a broken and hungry world, through the beauty or the cry of creation

Listen! Catch the rhythm of God's voice. Do you hear?

The fulfillment of vocation is celebration of life in God (*Blessed are you... Happy are you...*) — celebration that *is* life in God:

Blessed are the poor; blessed are the poor in spirit...
Blessed are those who mourn, blessed are the
comforters...
Blessed are those who hunger and thirst for justice...
Blessed are the peacemakers....

You are invited to the fullness of life. By stopping to listen, by nurturing right relationships, by moving to the margins, by ensconcing ourselves in communities committed to faithful discipleship, by living in harmony with the rest of creation — perhaps, just perhaps, we will catch the cadence of God's voice and hear the call or calls that are ours.

Notes

1. John Neafsey, *A Sacred Voice Is Calling* (Maryknoll, NY: Orbis Books, 2006), 5.

2. *Catechism of the Catholic Church*, no. 1717.

3. Ched Myers et al., *Say to This Mountain* (Maryknoll, NY: Orbis Books, 1996), 10.

4. Neafsey, *A Sacred Voice Is Calling*, 6.

5. Maria Harris, *Proclaim Jubilee!* (Louisville: Westminster John Knox Press, 1996), 25.

6. Synod of Bishops, *Justice in the World*, 1971.

7. Harris, *Proclaim Jubilee!*, 27.

8. Marie Dennis et al., *St. Francis and the Foolishness of God* (Maryknoll, NY: Orbis Books, 1993), chap. 4.

9. Ibid., 76.

10. Ibid., 77.

11. Ibid., 78.

12. Ibid., 79.

13. Neafsey, *A Sacred Voice Is Calling*, 26.

14. Dennis et al., *St. Francis and the Foolishness of God*, 34–36.

15. Neafsey, *A Sacred Voice Is Calling*, 30–31.

16. Dennis et al., *St. Francis and the Foolishness of God*, 110–11.

17. Ana Carrigan, *Salvador Witness: The Life and Calling of Jean Donovan* (Maryknoll, NY: Orbis Books, 2005).

18. SHARE, Prayer Service for 25th Anniversary of Four Church Women, 2005.

19. Ched Myers, *Binding the Strong Man* (Maryknoll, NY: Orbis Books, 1988), 132–33.

20. Ronald P. Hamel and Kenneth R. Himes, O.F.M., *Introduction to Christian Ethics: A Reader* (Mahwah, NJ: Paulist Press), 150.

21. Quoted in ibid., 195.

22. Neafsey, *A Sacred Voice Is Calling*, 3–4.

23. Marie Adele Dennis, *A Retreat with Oscar Romero and Dorothy Day* (Cincinnati: St. Anthony Messenger Press, 1997), 11–12.

24. *Catechism of the Catholic Church*, no. 1613.

25. 2006 UNAIDS' *Report on the Global AIDS Epidemic*.

26. Ched Myers et al., *Say to This Mountain* (Maryknoll, NY: Orbis Books, 1996), 15.

27. *Catechism of the Catholic Church,* no. 1719.

28. Ibid., no. 1723.

29. Ibid., no. 1717.

30. Pope Paul VI, *Populorum Progressio: On the Development of Peoples* (1967), no. 21.

31. *Catechism of the Catholic Church,* no. 1877.

32. *www.vitw.org.*

33. *www.cpt.org.*

34. *www.crs.org.*

35. Larry Rasmussen, *Earth Community Earth Ethics* (Maryknoll, NY: Orbis Books, 1996).

36. *www.earthcharter.org.*

37. *www.catholiccharitiesusa.org.*

38. *www.networklobby.org.*

39. *www.coc.org.*

40. *www.bread.org.*

41. *Rerum Novarum: The Condition of Labor,* 1891.

42. Edward DeBerri and James Hug, *Catholic Social Teaching: Our Best Kept Secret* (Maryknoll, NY: Orbis Books, 2003).

43. Bishops Synod Statement, *Justice in the World,* no. 6.

44. *Octogesima Adveniens: Call to Action,* no. 4.

45. *www.paxchristi.net.*

46. *www.paxchristiusa.org.*

47. *www.lffp.org.*

48. *www.ipj-ppj.org.*

49. *www.paceebene.org.*

50. *www.cpn.edu.*

51. *www.oikoumene.org/en/.*

52. *www.witnessforpeace.org.*

53. *Fire of Peace,* Pax Christi USA, 1992.

54. Ibid., no. 1717.

55. Jon Sobrino, *Witnesses to the Kingdom* (Maryknoll, NY: Orbis Books, 2003), 202–3.

56. *Catechism of the Catholic Church,* no. 1723.

57. Ibid., no. 1717.

58. Ibid., no. 1718.

59. Rasmussen, *Earth Community Earth Ethics,* 195ff.

60. *Catechism of the Catholic Church,* no. 1723.

61. Ibid., no. 1717.

"Truly a spirituality for the 21st century!"
— *Dolores Leckey*

Catholic Spirituality for Adults

General Editor
Michael Leach

Forthcoming volumes include:

+ *Charity* by Virgil Elizondo
+ *Listening to God's Word* by Alice Camille
+ *Community* by Adela Gonzalez
+ *Incarnation* by John Shea
+ And many others.

To learn more about forthcoming titles in the series, go to *orbisbooks.com*.

For free study guides and discussion ideas on this book, go to *www.rclbenziger.com*.

Please support your local bookstore.

Thank you for reading *Diversity of Vocations* by Marie Dennis. We hope you found it beneficial.